THE BOOK OF BEACONSFIELD

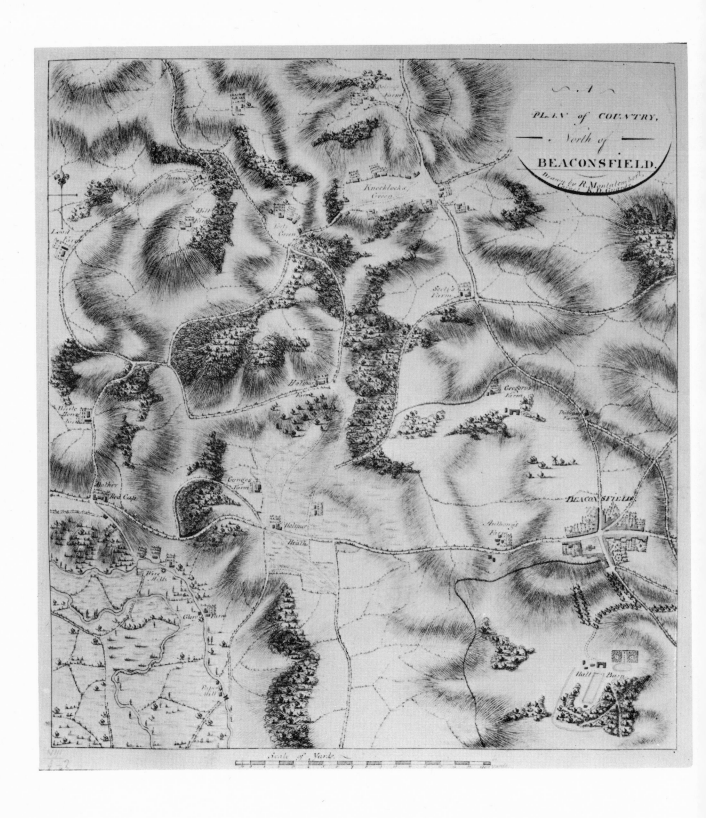

A late 18th century plan of the country north of Beaconsfield.
(British Library)

THE BOOK OF BEACONSFIELD

AN ILLUSTRATED RECORD

EDITED BY

CLIVE BIRCH

BARRACUDA BOOKS LIMITED
CHESHAM, BUCKINGHAMSHIRE, ENGLAND
MCMLXXVI

PUBLISHED IN THIS SECOND (1982) EDITION BY
BARRACUDA BOOKS LIMITED
BUCKINGHAM, ENGLAND
AND PRINTED BY
ROBENDENE LIMITED
AMERSHAM, ENGLAND

BOUND BY
HAZELL, WATSON & VINEY LIMITED
AYLESBURY, ENGLAND

JACKET PRINTED BY
CHENEY & SONS LIMITED
BANBURY, OXON

LITHOGRAPHY BY
SOUTH MIDLANDS LITHO PLATES LIMITED
LUTON, ENGLAND

TYPESET IN
MONOTYPE BASKERVILLE SERIES 169
BY SOUTH BUCKS TYPESETTERS LIMITED
BEACONSFIELD, ENGLAND

1982 AMENDMENTS TYPESET BY
BEDFORDSHIRE GRAPHICS LIMITED
BEDFORD, ENGLAND

ISBN 0 86023 012 0

Contents

Acknowledgments

In the first place, as Editor and co-author I wish to record my extensive obligation to my fellow authors, whose time, patience, knowledge and unfailing guidance and advice have made this book possible. Gerald Elvey has contributed the three major chapters on the town's origins and its history in the Tudor and Stuart periods—the first continuous record of the town's past yet published. In addition he and Elizabeth Elvey have guided me personally throughout my own researches and the editing of the book as a whole and have been instrumental in advising on the illustrations, and tracking down elusive material.

Bambi Stainton contributed the exhaustive survey of the town and its environs in the prehistoric eras, and located the relevant illustrations. Mrs Stainton was instrumental in encouraging me to undertake this book in the first place, and has spent many long hours advising me on related matters and introducing me to many other people who have helped in different ways.

Henry Reed researched and wrote the two chapters on poets and personalities of the town, and despite ill health, sought out and obtained some third of the illustrations in the book—many from hitherto unidentified sources. Mr Reed also undertook some of the research for the later chapters and has devoted many hours to assisting and advising me.

In addition, Mrs Kitty Holden kindly permitted me access to parochial records, and checked my own chapters, and my thanks are also due to Christopher Gowing and Rosemary Ewles of the County Museum, Jack Davis and Hugh Handley of the County Record Office, Colin Rippon and his staff at the County Reference Library, and to the Buckinghamshire Archaeological Society for help and advice in the identification and availability of relevant material.

During the extended period of preparation of this book, Roy Eden and his staff at Beaconsfield Library have shown unfailing courtesy and interest in handling the subscription facility, and Roy and Susanne Preece of Collection, and the Partners at Gallery 79 have kindly supported the book by holding subsidiary reservation facilities—without all these people the book could not have been published.

Arthur Church, Bernard Edwards and Tony White, Editors of the Bucks Free Press, Buckinghamshire Advertiser and Bucks Examiner, together with Eric Scott of Bucks Countryside have given the book continuous support.

Many residents of Beaconsfield have also helped, principally Dorothy Collins with material related to G. K. Chesterton and the Children's Convalescent Home, Rev Dr. J. S. Wright, Miss Fletcher and John Harding with many pictures. Dr. Gordon Wyatt has also kindly loaned a number of old prints from his personal collection.

Lord and Lady Burnham have throughout taken a keen interest in the book, and in particular made freely available information and illustrations of Hall Barn, also giving me unrestricted access to the house and grounds on numerous occasions. I am particularly indebted to Lord Burnham for contributing the Foreword.

Once again, I am indebted to my friend John Armistead for his painstaking work in reproducing the majority of the illustrations, working sometimes under difficult conditions and pressure of time.

Foreword

by Lieut-Col. the Lord Burnham

It is with great pleasure that I write to introduce Mr Clive Birch's 'Book of Beaconsfield'. To the best of my knowledge it is the first history of the town to achieve national publication.

We cannot in all honesty claim great fame for our town. We are not renowned for our art or our manufactures, and even the most distinguished of our past residents may be considered a little below the first rank in world history. Nevertheless it is the small towns which are the backbone of England and the repository of our native balance and common sense.

It is remarkable how much information can be passed down by oral tradition. One example is the Elizabethan wall paintings which were uncovered in No. 1 London End in 1966, and one of which is now preserved in the museum at Aylesbury. No resident living at that time had ever seen them, yet it was well known that they were there. However with the passage of time and a much more mobile population it is worth recording as much as possible of local history in a form more readily available than the original records.

I therefore wish this volume well and hope it will be of continuing interest to the present and future inhabitants of our town.

HALL BARN,
BEACONSFIELD.
May 1976.

Dedication

This book is dedicated to the library staffs of the town and county, who provide an essential service despite today's difficult conditions.

On Beaconsfield

(from three poems by G. K. Chesterton)

LINES ON A CRICKET MATCH

Come all; our land hath laurels too,
While round our beech-tree grows
The Shamrock of our exiled Burke
Or Waller's "lovely rose."

Who ever win or lose, our flags
Of fun and honour furled,
The glory of the game shall stand
Stonewalling all the world,

While those historic types survive
For England to admire
Twin pillars of our storied past,
The Burgess and the Squire.

from lines for an American friend

It is thousands of leagues, over land, over sea,
From Omaha City to Overroads door;
But we said: 'The great Prairies will leave (as they flee
Like infinite shadows)·the things that are sure.

We said: 'They are certain, the field or the friend,
From which we were far and of which we are fond,
That the donkeys still hammer down Aylesbury End
Or a dog is still drinking in Candlemas Pond."

from lines for Mrs Halford

Had we in London not in London End
   First seen you flame in footlights of renown
We had not dreamed what neighbour or what friend
   Could tread the tiny stages of our town.

A Town of Elegance

Beaconsfield, perhaps more than most of the towns of South Buckinghamshire, reflects its past in the face it presents to the outside world. Attractive to visitors and to many seeking a tranquil home within reach of the metropolis, it has retained the elegance it acquired in the 17th and 18th centuries without the soulless replanning of so many of its contemporaries. Yet the town has changed radically this century, mostly away from the original centre.

Until now, no continuous record of the town's past has been set down. In part this may be due to its relatively small size, but mainly perhaps because Beaconsfield has never suffered or enjoyed the upheavals of industry and commerce. Even today it is as it has been for some centuries, essentially a town for living in.

There is ample evidence of early activity in the area, but when settlement began, it was not here but in hamlets and estates throughout the district. The town as such was a relative latecomer, centred round the route to Oxford, and dependent upon the major estates. Burnham Abbey's dominance influenced the early settlement.

Gradually the prosperity that farming brought and the accessibility of the town created trade and the inns prospered too. Men of wit, means and fashion chose to live here, and they set the tone of the place. Community life developed during the Tudor period, and then the town we know began to emerge under the Stuarts.

Strangely, the road that established Beaconsfield reduced in importance and while Wycombe and Aylesbury thrived, Beaconsfield saw little apparent change, until in the 18th century early turnpike legislation brought the road sharply back into focus, and through traffic rapidly increased.

Throughout the 18th and 19th centuries the town developed its institutions. Then Beaconsfield once again avoided the changes that beset so much of the county, for the railway which burst into many towns mid-century and after, failed to reach this town until 1906. By then industry had followed the new metal tracks into other towns, so Beaconsfield escaped the industrial revolution.

When it did arrive, it brought rapid growth centred on the station, and the New Town was born, while the original centre remained relatively undisturbed. Multiple access to London, Midlands and the North once again attracted discerning residents, and today Beaconsfield reflects its past by its accessibility, its rural hinterland and its predominantly residential character.

This book is the story of the town, from earliest man's first visits to the community of today.

ABOVE: This early Stone Age man's flint hand axe was discovered at Seer Green. (Buckinghamshire County Museum and Archaeological Society—BCM)

RIGHT: A typical Neolithic pick found at Further Peggs, Jordans. (Mrs Wheen)

LEFT: New Stone Age man fashioned this miniature axe head, discovered at Hall Barn, Beaconsfield. (Dick Rolfe)

Before Beaconsfield

Long ago, Beaconsfield was submerged beneath the primeval sea. Gradually chalk was laid down until the land emerged, to be inundated once more, when clay, sand and pebbles collected on top of the chalk—fifty million years ago. When the waters receded, the Chilterns were the result. Beaconsfield itself lies on the wide plateau that slopes gently down to the south-east from the dramatic Chiltern escarpment.

Since then, these 'Reading Beds' have worn away, in places leaving patches of suitable clay for man's pot and tile making. Most of Penn stands on mottled clay, sand and pebbles, and the area is partly covered with plastic clay of the kind which promoted the 14th century Penn tile industry.

The Ice Ages of a million years ago and since also brought a grand mixture of debris to our slopes—even from as far away as Scandinavia. The area has been described as a geological dustbin, and is unlike any other chalk downland in the country, often varying, as people know, from garden to garden.

The resultant claylike soil below the scarp, often deep and ill drained, has influenced the plant life here, and one result is the beech—raw material for the most significant local industry, furniture. From the early bodgers to today's modern factories in nearby Wycombe, the product is heir to the Ice Age.

The Ice Age had other effects. Once the River Thames flowed further north, past Bourne End, Beaconsfield and Rickmansworth on its way to the East Anglian coastline, but the ice sheets forced it south, and it slipped down the chalk dip-slope. Perhaps the massive gravel deposits, just south of Beaconsfield and the A40 so important today not only to builders and roadmakers, but to most of our major industries, were laid down as a result.

But what of earliest man? If nature laid the groundwork for our landscape and forged the bases of our commerce, did the first primitive humans visit Beaconsfield? Certainly Primitive man was not far away 400,000 years ago, when the land bridge to the Continent had not yet been riven by the Channel. On the Thames gravels of that time, the famous Swanscombe skull came to rest. Over a long period, with the shift of those gravels nearer home, came the characteristic all purpose tools of the period—and several have been found locally.

Early Stone Age man hunted the rhinoceros, forest elephant, giant deer and the great wild ox, the auroch (not extinct until the 18th century), and he used pear shaped or oval flint hand axes. Five have surfaced here, one at Knotty Green, three at Long Bottom and Seer Green, and one at Beaconsfield itself.

The area formed part of the ice-bound lands of the last Ice Age, when Early Man hunted the horse, bison and reindeer herds that roamed our hillsides and plains, but once the ice retracted 10,000 years ago, his culture disappeared, and the land encouraged grass, then forest and finally today's beechwoods. Man adapted. The Middle Stone Age, or Mesolithic folk hunted these early forests for animals we would recognise—elk, deer, pig and smaller fry. Preferring to live by water, local hills were their hunting grounds, but they lived elsewhere. Their arrows, spears and clearing axes were tipped with worked flint, and one major local source was the valley that runs through Jordans, where many of their tools, together with quantities of their waste flint flakes, were dropped or discarded, to be found by their modern successors.

Six thousand years ago the sea rose as the ice melted, and Britain became an island. The European farming revolution was under way, and reached us about 4000 BC, Neolithic or New Stone Age man arriving by primitive boat and seeking fresh pastures. What he sought was light soil and an open landscape or well drained gravel, and that's what the Chilterns and Thames Valley offered; he cleared our woodlands though he found our soils pocked with stone.

Seer Green saw his passing, and there he left certain evidence: flint arrowheads. He also left them at Jordans, just where thousands of years before, his predecessors made their tools. Neolithic implements and waste flint flakes have been found in quantity in the dry valley floor that runs down from Seer Green and Jordans, past Bulstrode to Hedgerley.

Now Neolithic man cleared the forests, and the sort of axe he used is the polished one he left behind at Wilton Park, and the smaller find on the Hall Barn estate.

Early in the second millenium, the Beaker Folk arrived in South Bucks, bringing with them their characteristic pottery vessels and a knowledge of metalworking. They mixed with the natives and a more sophisticated culture developed. They left their memoranda along the escarpment and in local valleys. There are to be seen their burial mounds and of their metal artefacts, it was once claimed that a bronze sword was found in a rabbit scrape on the Bulstrode estate. Our only evidence today is of their barbed and tanged hunting arrowheads, made of flint and perhaps fired at some animal and lost where the Bell House Hotel and Grove Road now stand.

Still, if each culture since the earliest men has visited us, the evidence, if not our observation of it, is sparse. But Beaconsfield boasts at least one mystery monument—The Mount, in the midst of woodlands on the Beaconsfield golf course. Never investigated, it has been the basis of countless speculations. Is it a Bronze Age barrow, or a beacon? There are others like it on vantage points elsewhere in the area. Some say the town's name is thus derived— 'a field with a beacon', rather than the commonly accepted 'field in the beechwoods'.

The weather deteriorated and after 650 BC the development of Iron Age culture faced more intractable conditions, less conducive to farming. Hill forts protected land against the heightened competition for a suitable settlement, and earthworks encircle Chiltern hilltops such as that at Cholesbury, near Chesham, and lower, circular earthworks are evident such as that at Bulstrode Park, and the remnants of one at Moat Farm, north of Hedgerley—largely destroyed by gravel working and the M40 motorway construction. This is thought to have been a defensive work, not a homestead moat, and probably an Iron Age Plateau Fort.

Iron Age man left one known reminder of his presence in Beaconsfield—pottery in Stratton road. Then the Belgic peoples invaded, Celtic tribes such as the Catuvellauni, who focussed on the Chilterns, fought Caesar in 55 and 54 BC and left traces of their settlements at Burnham, Saunderton, Cholesbury and throughout the Chess valley.

These were the people who introduced money, and one hoard only has been retrieved in South Bucks—in 1826 at High Wycombe. Eleven gold staters of Tasciovanus, ruler of the Catuvellauni, were tucked away in an Iron Age moneybox, a hollowed flint.

With the Roman conquest of 43 AD the now indigenous tribes adapted, and accepted the orderly administration and land division of the new regime. Romanised inhabitants raised villas on their estates, and nearby river valleys boast many at regularly spaced intervals. But the uplands were irrelevant to the new way of life, and Beaconsfield was not favoured. However, local clay was important, and a cluster of pottery kilns were built at Hedgerley, Fulmer and Gerrards Cross in the 2nd century AD—we have yet to discover where the clay workers lived.

Communications underpinned the Romano-British culture, and the newcomers were first class road engineers. While their major roadworks are still with us in essence in many areas, most local roads would have been simply metalled ways and beaten tracks, long since gone. But one major road appears to have been driven right through Beaconsfield, linking Verulamium (St Albans) with Silchester. Traced by The Viatores as far as Chalfont St Giles, it would have crossed Wilton Park and Hall Barn before crossing the Thames at Hedsor. Local place and field names containing the words street, stone or stane, reinforce its presence. The 4th century AD was the golden age of Roman Britain, but in 407 AD the legions left, and Britain—and South Bucks—was left to cope as best it could with the increasing interference of barbarians from all quarters.

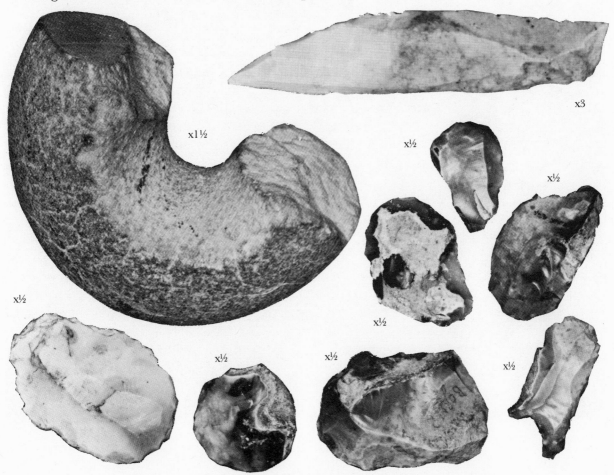

Remnants of the Stone Age cultures—LEFT: part of a pebble macehead found off Twitchells lane, Jordans, (Mrs Wheen); RIGHT: a Mesolithic point from Further Peggs, Jordans (Mrs Wheen), and BELOW: Stone Age flint scrapers from Jordans, and from Wattleton and Penn roads Beaconsfield. (Mrs Wheen and Mrs Stainton)

ABOVE LEFT: This barb and tang arrowhead from the early Bronze Age surfaced at Jordans, while CENTRE: Pot Kiln lane yielded this Neolithic leaf arrowhead and RIGHT: its Stone Age fellow was found at Grove Road with its barbs broken. (All Dick Rolfe)

BELOW: The Mount, Beaconsfield—did it give the town its name?

16

ABOVE: The Romans left plenty of evidence of their 130-170 AD pottery factory near Hedgerley, south of Wapsey's Wood. BELOW: Some of their local pots survived. (Records of Bucks)

17

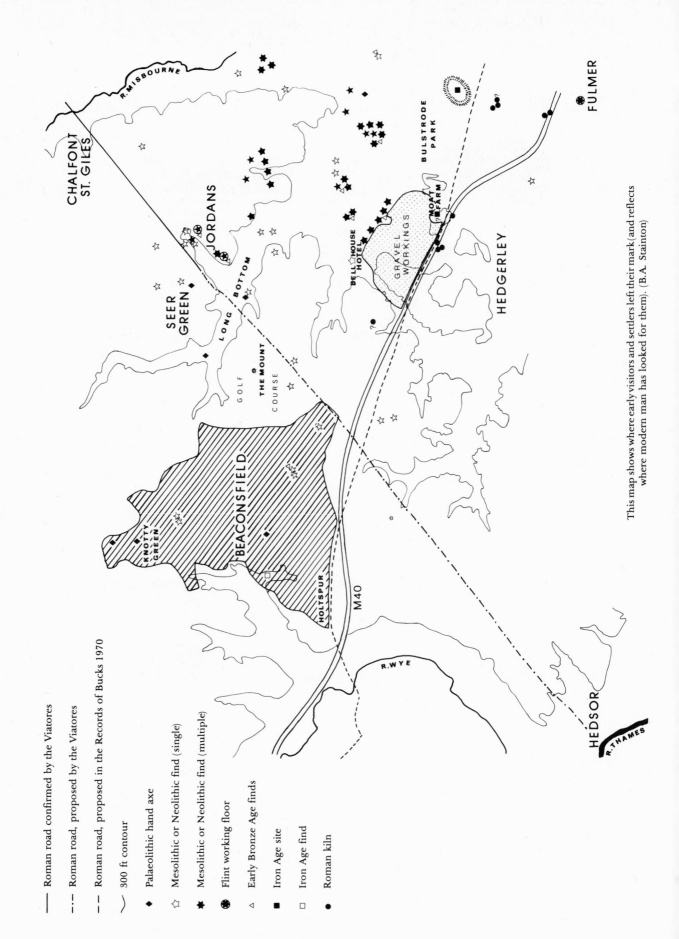

CHALFONT ST. GILES

R.MISBOURNE

JORDANS

SEER GREEN

LONG BOTTOM

BELL HOUSE HOTEL

BULSTRODE PARK

GRAVEL WORKINGS

MOAT FARM

HEDGERLEY

FULMER

GOLF COURSE

THE MOUNT

KNOTTY GREEN

BEACONSFIELD

HOLTSPUR

M40

R.WYE

HEDSOR

R.THAMES

This map shows where early visitors and settlers left their mark (and reflects where modern man has looked for them). (B.A. Stainton)

Roman road confirmed by the *Viatores*

Roman road, proposed by the *Viatores*

Roman road, proposed in the Records of Bucks 1970

300 ft contour

◆ Palaeolithic hand axe

☆ Mesolithic or Neolithic find (single)

★ Mesolithic or Neolithic find (multiple)

✪ Flint working floor

△ Early Bronze Age finds

■ Iron Age site

□ Iron Age find

● Roman kiln

Mediaeval Scene

The Saxon invaders settled in the river valleys, siting their villages on the alluvial land close to the smaller rivers—the Wye, Misbourne and Colne, but in the Thames valley on the gravel shelf above it. The large upland tract above these four valleys was then, and for long afterwards unappropriated. The men who lived in the valleys, and others from farther afield, as we shall see, used it in common; it was for the most part scrub and heath, with intermittent woodland—valuable for pasturing cattle in winter and spring, and for feeding swine. When the land came to be needed for arable farming, the whole area was parcelled out among the villages that had previously commoned there. These are the conclusions that we must draw from a study of the map as it was until it was 'tidied up' early in Queen Victoria's reign. The villages in the Thames valley all had shares in the upland, some of them detached and remote from their parents: Hedgerley Bulstrode was in Upton, Hedgerley was in Eton, Penn was part of Taplow. Most of Beaconsfield fell to the share of Burnham, but the northern part, together with Coleshill in Amersham, was obtained by the men of Wigginton and Tring, and so became part of Hertfordshire.

No date can be assigned to these happenings, for we are dependent on circumstantial in the absence of direct evidence, but it would be reasonable to suppose that it was the land-hunger of Scandinavian invaders with Danegeld in their purses that led to these early enclosures, and that the development of this area began in the tenth century. None of the newer villages is mentioned by name in Domesday Book, though they can mostly be identified within the parent village. We must wait indeed for another century before the name of Beaconsfield first emerges; at the end of the twelfth century, however, a number of land transactions took place here, and gave rise to documents which tell us much about the parish and how it had been developed, and from then onwards an abundance of private deeds reveal many of the changes in the ownership of land which occurred over the next three centuries. These documents, as a great historian once said, are very taciturn: they don't yield up their secrets easily; yet from them all much can be learned, and a story comes into being which is an unusual one, not quite on all fours with those of the older villages.

Those in the valleys were nucleated villages: each was the nucleus of an agricultural unit with common arable fields tilled by the lord and all the villagers, surrounded by meadow and pasture. Beaconsfield was not developed after this manner: what appears to have come into being is a number of hamlets, each of which consisted of three, or occasionally two farms, with their dependent cottages adjacent. It is possible that at the outset the lands of each hamlet were cultivated in common and the produce divided and that later on the land itself was divided, so that each farmer held in severalty, though the land remained in common fields. Finally, however, and mostly towards the end of the period we are considering, the lands of each hamlet were divided afresh so that the land of every farmer could be totally enclosed, and lie in a fairly compact block.

These hamlets were not closely knit: the farms did not lie cheek by jowl as in a nucleated

19

village. The Alder Ridge for example—Woodlands Farm, the cradle of the Aldridge family —together with Holloways and a farm called Aldremere which lay on the other side of the road but has long disappeared leaving little trace, formed one such hamlet, and others can be worked out.

The terms on which the lord had originally granted land to these farmers cannot be known, but at the end of the twelfth century some of the tenures were free and some unfree. The unfree tenancies assured the lord of labour to till his home farm, to reap his harvest and to mow his hay. The unfree tenants had this compensation for their status that however bad the season might be they could always work with their hands, and were far less likely to lose their holdings in hard years than they would have been if they had been paying the rent in coin. However that may be, it seems that during the earlier thirteenth century the unfree tenants all became freemen and long before its end we cease to hear of villeins or villein tenures. In 1293, Richard de la Holeweye, who was undoubtedly a descendant of the Laurence de la Holeweye who held there unfreely in 1200, made a charter giving to his brother 'all the livestock in my manor, and all my boxes, coffers and court-chests'. Gregory, who belongs to the second quarter of the thirteenth century and gave his name to that farm, was always a freeman, as were his parents; his mother bore a Scandinavian name. The Grove, in all probability the Seelys of today, was in 1200 held by Robert de la Grave unfreely, but his descendants were among the most prosperous and respected people in Beaconsfield. A famous French historian, comparing the men that lived in uplands, farming individual farms, with those who tilled the common fields of the older villages, thought there was evidence to show that the upland men excelled in self-reliance and sturdy independence of mind and spirit.

It was, moreover, no isolated existence that they led. With London close at hand, with four boroughs within a few miles, and with travellers passing to and fro through the town, their lives cannot have lacked variety. They frequently had to attend courts of law or official enquiries, as parties, witnesses or jurors—sometimes at unwelcome distances from home. Those who sought wider travel could join a pilgrimage, having mortgaged their lands to pay the travel-agent, but the attendant dangers were manifold and great. Simon son of John, who held what is now Overs Farm of Robert Glorie, returned safe from Compostella in the summer of 1214 to learn that his brother Geoffrey had brought suit against Robert, claiming the farm as next heir, and not only alleging that he had died on the pilgrimage but producing a witness who testified that he had been present at his death. Fortunately for Simon, the case had been adjourned, and he managed to get to London in time to walk into court when it was called on again.

We must now turn round for a moment to take a look at the lords. The fiefs of the twenty knights whose service the barony of Windsor owed to the king, and whose duty it was to guard Windsor Castle when need arose, were for the most part grouped tightly round it; at the time of Domesday, however, the Buckinghamshire lands—Burnham (in which Beaconsfield was situated) and Eton (which included Wexham and Hedgerley)—remained in the possession of the baron himself. Walter son of Other was then the holder of the barony; his father had held land in Hampshire before the Conquest, and was no doubt of Saxon or Scandinavian descent. Other must have held the same position and the same estates: the place-name Othershacche—the gate of Other's home farm—occurs in our early records.

During the next forty years or so, an estate was created here for Reginald, one of Walter's younger sons, who thus became one of the knights of the barony, and our first resident squire. That is not to say that he always lived here, for he had another preoccupation: he assisted his brother Maurice to exercise the office of steward to the abbey of St Edmund at Bury and administer its vast estates and interests in East Anglia. It is highly probable that this was a family of literate laymen. The new estate centred on the farm that later became Wiltons. By no means the whole of Beaconsfield was given to Reginald: the baronial demesne was retained, with its manor house and grange. The manor house most probably stood where Hall Place later stood—the present rectory; its grange where Hall Barn now is.

Manorial descents are notoriously tiresome pursuits, but the subsequent history of both estates must be briefly noticed. The barony of Windsor was partitioned, at the end of the twelfth century, between William III and Walter II; Walter obtained Beaconsfield, and on his death without issue in 1201 it passed to his two sisters, Gunnora the wife of Hugh de Hodeng and Christine the wife of Duncan de Lascelles. There we can leave that story for a while.

Reginald de Burnham left Robert, son and heir, who had two sons, Robert and Hugh. The second Robert added considerably to his patrimony by further acquisitions in Beaconsfield from Walter II de Windsor and Ralf son of Hugh de Hodeng, until, apart from the demesne farm (which then or at any rate shortly afterwards came to be called Hallebarne), he owned virtually the whole parish, receiving money rents from the various farmers, and himself residing at Wiltons and farming there; the great ditch that he made round a hundred acres of heath which he purchased and brought under the plough is still for the most part intact. When he was an old man he retired into the infirmary at Missenden Abbey, and there he died and was buried. He gave to the abbey the lands that he had bought; the rents receivable from them proved, however, to be customary rents which could not be increased as the value of money declined, and they became of less significance as the years went by. When Robert died in 1224 he left no children, and his brother Hugh, who was one of the Canons of St Paul's, succeeded him. Hugh had been a married man, for in his younger days clerical marriages were quite usual, and his son Hugh was his recognised heir, not only to the lands in Beaconsfield but to his stall in St Paul's, and he also became archdeacon of Colchester. He in turn had a son Hugh, but times had changed, and the condemnation of clerical marriage by Pope and by Council made it difficult for sons of the clergy to be admitted into their fathers' estates. The young Hugh was set up by the archdeacon at Dernedene, now Pennlands, which then acquired a sub-manorial status; Hugh held a court to which his tenants owed suit. On the archdeacon's death the de Burnham lordship passed to his two aunts; one of them, who was married to William de Hedsor, later obtained the whole.

How early there was a church here is not known, but at the beginning of the thirteenth century there was one in existence on the present site. Its being referred to as a *monasterium* is no evidence for there having been a monastery or monastic cell here, for the word was quite commonly used to denote a parish church—nor is there any other evidence. At first it was a chapelry of Burnham Church, whose rector, apparently after consultation with the lord of the de Burnham fee, appointed a vicar to minister in it: the first recorded appointment was of the rector's son, who undertook to make a handsome yearly payment to his father out of the revenue. In these circumstances it is not surprising that there was no glebe here, but from the first the vicars seem to have had the whole tithe and the offerings. During the course of the thirteenth century the Hodengs successfully asserted their right to present the vicar, who in the early fourteenth became a rector.

Not only was the parish almost entirely under cultivation in thriving farms, but its principal hamlet lay at the crossing of two important roads, the road to Oxford and thence to Gloucester and through Wales to St David's, and that which led from the crossing of the Thames at Windsor to Aylesbury, Buckingham and the Watling Street at Stony Stratford or Towcester. Beaconsfield was not, in the Middle Ages, one of the recognised stages on the Oxford road: these were Uxbridge, Wycombe and Tetbury. Yet both these roads must have brought trade and wealth; the inns that were developed here were a source of prosperity to the whole parish: they provided employment and they afforded a valuable outlet for the best of the farm products. As early as 1242 an inn and its host were mentioned to the justices at an assize:

> 'A merchant from overseas was entertained at the house of Peter de Winchendon in the town of Beaconsfield, and as he was leaving that house he was robbed by one of his own men. It is not known who that man was, nor even what his name was, so nothing further. Peter, attached for the robbery, came and is not suspected.'

A little later on, a development occurred which caused repercussions here. Thomas de Lascelles, whose mother had brought him half the lordship of Burnham and Beaconsfield drifted during the 1250s into low financial water. He may well have mortgaged these lands to one of the Jews whose assets Henry III had given to his brother Richard, earl of Cornwall and King of the Romans. At any rate all these Lascelles lands were at first mortgaged, and then sold to the earl, who appears at the same time to have acquired the Hodeng share of Beaconsfield as well, excepting the church, the title to which was hardly yet established enough to make it a saleable commodity.

No sooner were these transactions completed than the earl obtained from the king a licence to hold a weekly market in his manor of Beaconsfield. The establishment of a market naturally tended to bring greater prosperity, most of all perhaps to the inns and taverns, but none the less for that to the community at large. The lord would benefit in general from the betterment of his tenants, and in particular from the tolls that he charged on the goods that were sold there and the fees that he drew from the court that his steward held for the settlement of trading disputes. The eventual intention may have been the foundation of a borough, but that step was never taken, perhaps because there were so many boroughs all round—Wycombe, Marlow, Amersham, Denham and Uxbridge all within a few miles.

The reason, on the other hand, may be of a different sort, namely that Richard had already resolved upon a project which he brought to fruition in 1265 with the foundation on the site of the Lascelles manor-house in Burnham of an abbey of Austin nuns, and its endowment with the Lascelles and Hodeng lands that he had acquired here. The abbess of Burnham became the lady of Beaconsfield.

It is easy to attribute more importance to this event than it merits. By the time it took place, the lord had very little land left in demesne: the residue that had remained half a century before had been largely dissipated. All the land in the manor, which was almost coterminous with the parish, paid rent, but most of the rents were quit-rents, paid in acknowledgement of the lordship and not as representing the value of the holdings. What was of most value to the abbess were the courts she was entitled to hold—her manorial court (in theory every three weeks), and the courts of pie-powder at the markets and the annual fair which in 1269 the King granted her the right to hold. The change of ownership made little difference to the tenants: very probably the steward who had served the Lascelles and Hodengs was taken over by the earl and passed into the service of the abbey. The tenants were largely self-governing; their rents were regulated by manorial custom with which the law did not often interfere.

22

If we place ourselves, say in 1325, and look about, we shall see the Gregorys, the Groves, the Whites, the Syreds, the Dernedenes and the rest of them farming lands that have been developed to the full: not much heath is left now, and so little woodland that what remains is eagerly sought after, and quite small parcels are bought and ditched round. The town is beginning to take on a more modern shape: the Ends are expanding and beginning to creep outwards. The presence of a trading community is clear from the surnames that occur in our documents—Chapman, Cobbler, Ironmonger, Wheeler. The most lucrative and important of all the trades that were then carried on here was the manufacture of tiles. Members of the Penn family had been established in Dernedene in the mid-thirteenth century, and their name remains there. Near by, and no doubt engaged in the same business, lived successive members of the family of Alkeshulle; John de Alkeshulle, grandson of the first one we hear of, was the king's purveyor, not only of tiles but of building materials of every sort, and even of ships' timbers. He had the right of preemption in every county in England, and it was his duty to agree the price, and then send the materials wherever they were needed—to Westminster, to Windsor, to Bristol and even to Calais—certifying the bill for payment at the Exchequer. He died about 1364, having served the king and his father for the past forty years.

A windmill is first heard of in a lawsuit in 1311, but the indications are that it had been in existence for some time. In the early thirteenth century, most lords whose manors lay on uplands built windmills, and Robert II de Burnham, who as we have seen put considerable capital into this manor, probably built this mill, and it must have been a profitable investment. If the cost of multure was comparable to that of the Wycombe or Wooburn mills, the savings of cartage down and up the long steep hills advantaged the tenants greatly.

The ease of access from all over the south of the county made the town a favourite place for the transaction of civil and ecclesiastical business. The itinerant court of the archdeacon, a principal function of which was the proving of wills, often came to Beaconsfield, and its proceedings would take place in the church. The king's justices, when they came into the county, sat at Wycombe, Aylesbury and Newport, but the sheriff and his officers, who were perpetually summoning juries to enquire into this and that, found it an excellent point of assembly, and their business could be despatched at an inn or an alehouse.

Two of the farming families, the Groves and the Gregorys, had by now formed connexions in the city of London, and from the thirteenth century onwards younger sons were sometimes given a portion or a loan during their fathers' lifetime in order that they might, after an apprenticeship, set themselves up in trade there. Adam, the second son of Richard atte Grove, prospered in London (where he was known as Adam of Beaconsfield) enough to enable him to return and purchase an estate in Chalfont St Giles that was being sold to repay a mortgage; it has been called the Grove ever since. Adam and his descendants continued to trade in London for two hundred years and more; the last male heir, Roger de la Grove, was Master of the Grocers' Company in the early years of the sixteenth century. They retained the Grove, however, and kept up their connexion with their kinsmen in Beaconsfield. Another younger son, Laurence Gregory, became a citizen of London, and evidently throve there, because he was able to buy two houses in London End here, as well as some farmland, and he had money to lend on mortgages. Here, as elsewhere, a very usual source of finance was the rector or vicar; certainly Geoffrey of Haveringdown in the thirteenth century, and Ralf Badelkyng in the fourteenth were carrying on business as financiers.

Some important changes occurred at this time. Wiltons had passed from the Hedsors to

Richard de la Vache of Chalfont St Giles, who had greatly enriched himself during the Barons' Wars; he used it to provide for his second son Walter. When the cadet family died out, the estate was bought, in about 1340, by Thomas de Whelton, from whom its name derives. Though Thomas had lands elsewhere, this must have been a principal residence, for he obtained from Bishop Burghersh a licence for mass to be celebrated in the private chapel there.

The Hyde, which was also a considerable property but whose previous history is obscure, was purchased about 1325 by Ralf de Wedon, of Wedonhill in Amersham, who had lands in other places in the county, and served three times as its sheriff. It was, however, again in the market after his death, and it was then acquired by another and more successful royal servant. Sir Hugh de Berewyk, whose forebears probably came from Berrick in Oxfordshire, was employed in administrative and judicial business, mainly in the Duchy of Lancaster, of which he rose to become the steward. These duties kept him at most times in the north of England, but later on he was much employed on judicial business in this and neighbouring counties. He set to work to build up a great estate in Beaconsfield: he bought Harrias in the next year, and Wiltons the year after that. Most important of all, he bought the de Burnham lordship, and the demesne farm at Hall Barn. Other farms and numerous parcels of land all over the parish fell to him in course of time, and within ten years or so he was not only the lord but the possessor of most of Beaconsfield.

But by no means all: an indigenous competitor watched the market from day to day. Richard Gregory makes his first appearance in our records in 1321, and for the last time in 1385. He was in practice as a lawyer—one of that long succession of Beaconsfield lawyers that can be traced from before his time till our own century. He was elected a coroner for the county, and frequently commissioned for judicial business. He acted for Sir Hugh de Berewyk when he bought the Hyde. Though it is not possible to say just what he owned at the close of his long life, nor even to identify most of the parcels of land that he acquired, his estate here was certainly the next in importance to Sir Hugh's. In several of the surrounding villages he also had land. His heir was his son Richard, from whom it passed to Gregory Ballard the king's butler, whose father had married the old man's daughter.

The Black Death appears to have assailed us with great ferocity in March 1349. Few of the names that occurred with regularity in the charters of the preceding ten years can be seen again after that precise date; some family names vanish altogether. Our information, however, is insufficient to permit us to concoct even the most rudimentary statistics. This mortality, and the changed social conditions that flowed from it, must have brought much land on to the market, usually to be snapped up and added to the Berewyk or the Gregory estate.

Thomas, the last male Berewyk, died in 1416, and his lands passed to his sister Margaret, the wife of Ralph Butler of Badminton in Gloucestershire. The Berewyks had probably lived in Beaconsfield—it was no more usual in those days than it is now for wealthy men to live always in one house—but the only Butler known to have played a part in the life of this county was John, Ralph's son, who was a knight of the Shire and served twice as its sheriff. After his death in 1477, the estate seems to have been let to Robert Bulstrode and then to his son Sir William.

Wiltons, however, was not included in this arrangement. At some date, perhaps at this time, it passed into the leasehold tenure of the Wallers, who appeared on the scene for the first time in 1472, when John Waller was the last of five witnesses to a deed; it is likely that he was the lawyer responsible for drafting it. Very little is known about this John Waller, except that he married a Widmer, and that the Widmers were for generations a legal family.

Other men of consequence came to settle here in or before the fifteenth century, and took a prominent part in local affairs. The Gardiners, always citizens of London, were here before the middle of that century, and remained to the third generation; they appear to have taken a lease of Gregories but to have resided in and carried on the King's Head, where we shall meet one of them presently. The Browns, who arrived here, also from London, in Richard II's reign, acquired, perhaps then, the Saracen's Head and the George. When William Brown died in 1487 he left both these houses to his brother John, together with his lease of a brewery in London, so that perhaps we have here an early instance of a tied house. Another newcomer was Frank 'Pateinmaker', a 'Dutchman', who came from Louvain, and had obtained a royal licence to stay within the realm for life, providing he was of good behaviour. It is likely that an attraction of Beaconsfield for men with capital and trading ambition lay in its not being a borough, where restrictions imposed by a ruling oligarchy in its own interests would hamper a newcomer and prevent his developing a profitable business. However that may be, the fact is that whereas, a century before, there had been a dribble of emigrants from here into London, the observable flow seems now to be in the contrary direction.

The Domesday Survey of 1086 records Burnham, (BCM).

25

ABOVE LEFT: Beckensfeild Church.
ABOVE RIGHT: The boss of arms of Richard, Earl of Cornwall.
BELOW : Burnham   Priory.

26

Duncan de Lascelles and Christian his wife give land to Wix Priory,
Duncan, who was a Yorkshireman, became the owner of Beaconsfield in his wife's right in 1200 and died in 1208, so the charter, which is not dated, falls into that period. He gives them: (1) the homage of Alard son of Aldwin with all his progeny, and half the land of Deue (later called Wiggenton Farm); (2) The heath lying between Deue and the chalk-pit and between the church and Other's gate; (3) Half the park which was Walter de Windsor's in Beaconsfield, excepting Aldwin's land. This is a gift in exchange for other land. Within twenty years Alard had become a freeman. This is our earliest surviving charter. (By permission of The Controller, H.M. Stationery Office).

The grandson of a serf becomes a lord

Richard son of Hugh de la Holeweye grants to Eustace his brother all the live stock in his manor in Beaconsfield; also all his boxes, coffers and court-chests, several vats, and all the rest of the vessels, great and small, in the said manor. 8 May 1293. Our earliest dated charter. Lambert de la Holeweye, who held Holloways in 1200, was a villein, and it must have been a source of pride to Richard to be able, in the presence of his principal neighbours, to describe his farm as a manor. The second witness, William the clerk, was an early lawyer practising here. Clerk may be already a surname rather than descriptive. Osbert de la Brome is the grandson of Alard son of Aldwin of the first charter. (Bodleian Library).

The Old Crown lies concealed behind the facade of
Burke's Lodge, London End.

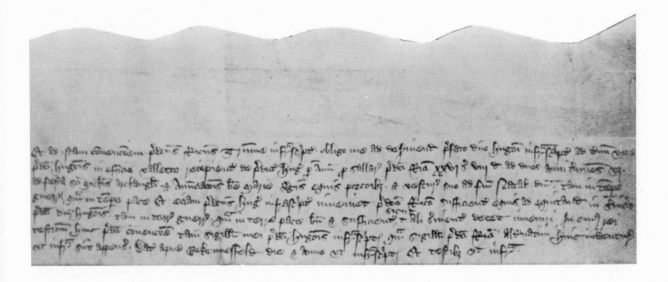

Sir Hugh de Berewyk engages a groom

Richard Grum of Harrow agrees to serve as groom during Sir Hugh's lifetime for 26s 8d yearly, in war and in peace. Sir Hugh will find sufficient horses for him to ride in his service, as he ought to do for a servant of his standing, and livery at Christmas every year. Further, Sir Hugh grants to R.G., Emma his wife and William their son, for their lives and the life of the longest liver, a cottage nearby, and a little farm that had belonged to John Shepherd (who probably gave his name to Shepherd's Lane), for 13s 4d yearly. "If Sir Hugh shall die before Richard (which God forbid), then Richard shall not pay the 13s 4d, on account of his faithful service." 25 March 1387. (Bodleian Library).

A farm changes hands

Isabel Basse sells her farm, lock stock and barrel, to an outsider, John Ledbourn of Denham. 7 October 1330.
Times had been very hard indeed during the last few years, and much land was being forced on to the market in consequence.

The Black Death takes its toll

Alexander Ledburgh of Denham conveys to Richard Gregory the elder all his property in Beaconsfield which he inherited when his uncle John Ledburgh died. 12 September 1349.
The great plague had come this way in March of that year, and it had evidently carried off John Ledburgh and any family that he had. It is strange that nineteen years of residence were long enough to imprint the name of this man on our map. The farm seems to have been mainly to the north of Ledborough Lane, that is to say in Hertfordshire. (Both Bodleian Library).

30

Tudor Town and Country

When the curtain rises for the second act, our attention is drawn to a different part of the scene, for the sources we have been relying on have largely dried up, though others, equally authentic but more difficult to assemble and use, have taken their place. Throughout the middle ages, we have depended in the main on deeds recording transfers of land, supported sometimes by scraps from the Public Records. For the Tudor and Stuart periods, comparatively few deeds are accessible, but fortunately we are well compensated by the survival of a large number of registered wills. These are only, of course, a small proportion of all that were made, for it was still a Christian duty to make a will, even for a woman, who in law owned nothing—so that her will could take no effect without her husband's consent. It was not a necessity to register a will, for it became valid in law when it was proved in the Church court, but where lands passed, it was prudent to do so, or when it gave rise to long-enduring trusts or to the likelihood of disputes. Some wills, for the sake of economy, were registered only in part, for the cost varied with the length.

None the less, though many of these wills are baffling and disappointing documents, yet the totality of them all—about a hundred and fifty up to the Civil War—sheds quite a lot of light on the scene. The testators were of all sorts and conditions—landowners, farmers, lawyers, inn and alehouse keepers, manufacturers, traders, labourers, and women, married and unmarried, of all degrees; there is only one clergyman among them, Richard Caple, curate of the parish, who died in 1500 leaving the then handsome sum of 40s towards the building of the new Church House which still survives.

The deeds recording men's purchases and sales reveal nothing of themselves or their motives, but the wills and testaments by which they passed their lands and possessions to their families are personal records, however formal their wording may be. As we read them, we feel we are present with them at a poignant moment, when death is before their eyes, yet despite the pain they suffer they must give final shape to plans long pondered and discussed, on which the futures of their children will depend. 'I, William Bulstrode, knight, lying in my deathbed', says one testator in 1526, writing his will with his own hand, and most of them might have said the same. The names of the witnesses are transcribed, so that we can see that with us in the room is often the rector (so we know which of them resided), a lawyer, one or two of the family, and perhaps a servant.

The wills of the menfolk do not usually tell us much about their goods, for these probably went to the widow for her life, and there was no need to list them, but she often had discretion as to their disposal, so that her will would mention every article and its recipient. Yet some men's goods represented their fortunes, and others took particular pride in certain items. Joan Bedyll, widow of a farmer or grazier, when she died in 1539, left to each of twelve grandchildren a sheet and a pewter dish; to five children of Arthur Stonall five sheep each; to other legatees a sheet and a candlestick, a black cow, a little kettle, 'my great brass pot', and to 'Cycyly Ball', the poet Waller's grandmother, 'the little bed that lieth on the

31

truckle bed'. John Gardiner owned the King's Head, and died there in 1507, while he was in course of making great improvements to it. He left to his lawyer-accountant 'my great spit of iron, with the iron cupboard belonging thereto'. To Margery Robyns of Seelys, his sister, he left his great cauldron, together with two vats of twenty gallons and more, in order that she might pray for his soul. William Axtell, who died in 1541, was a prosperous wheel-wright; he left to his son William, who succeeded him in trade, 300 of ashen timber as it lies, 1000 spokes as they rise, a table, a cupboard, two axes and an auger. To his son Robert he left all the presses, so presumably William had to take him into partnership. Richard Nedham, a smith, died in 1567 leaving no child; he lists his working tools, which are few, and leaves them to a nephew; to a cousin he left three dozen horse-shoes and 400 horse nails. Edward Boulton, in 1624, left to his son his working tools with all the swords, daggers and other weapons. The wealthy left silver and plate; Robert Waller, in 1545, left a piece to nearly every one of his children; Sir William Bulstrode left to the archbishop of Canterbury, who was to be overseer of his will, his best standing cup—a sumptuous one, no doubt; but the most remarkable possession of all was surely bequeathed by Robert Lee in 1572 to his friend Thomas Hewghes—'my unicorn's horn'.

It is in contrast to the preceding period that the limelight now falls on the town rather than on the countryside. Not only were the testators mostly resident there, but some of those who rented or acquired farms commuted into the town to carry on business there. Robert Waller had a lease, perhaps the same lease that his father had enjoyed, of Wiltons, but he does not seem to have lived there; Richard Tredway, the lawyer, at the end of the century, lived at Gregories; Richard Gosnold, who married his daughter and succeeded him in practice, acquired Overs. But the principal reason why we hear less about the farms is that by then it had become a general usage among ordinary farmers to convey their lands to trustees during their lifetime, directing them to pass the lands of their inheritance to the heir at their death, and land bought during their lifetime for that purpose to the younger children; no testamentary disposition was needed.

In these circumstances it is difficult to say what was going on on the farms. Over the country at large the general tendency during the later fifteenth century and the earlier sixteenth was for land to go down to grass, principally in aid of sheep-farming, but also to provide meat for the towns. The impression one derives from these wills is that much land that had once been ploughed was now grazed. Bequests of animals are commoner than of grain. In the mid-fifteenth century, Thomas Admond, butcher of Beaconsfield was active in the provisioning of Calais. The Graces, graziers on a large scale and traders in meat in London, settled down here, as did the Coblonds, graziers also. It may have been an attractive offer from a grazier that had caused John Robyns of Seelys, whose mother we have met, to lease his farm, reserving for himself only a 'chamber, the going of two beasts summer and winter, and half the fruit growing on all my ground'. Such, at all events was the state of affairs at Seelys when he made his will in 1546. (He left all his land to Edith, the elder of his two daughters, at 21. Three years later, she was married to William Cely, very probably the son of a William Cely who had been in the service of Sir William Bulstrode, and by him most generously provided for. Yet another William Cely, doubtless the son or grandson of this marriage, died in possession of the farm in 1606, leaving as his heir another Edith, this time only two years old).

Only two of the families that had been farming here in the early thirteenth century when our records begin were still on their farms in the sixteenth. The Aldridges have already been mentioned; Woodlands passed from one to another, each in his turn well to the fore in local affairs. When Robert Aldridge died in 1613 he was content to be described in his will as a husbandman, but his son Henry, who died five years later, was styled 'gentleman', and so were his successors. A prosperous cadet branch held the White Hart until the 1620s, when it was sold to Robert Stanborough. Another family of equal, if not greater antiquity was that of Stonall, which derived its name from the Stonehall in Chalfont St Giles (now Stonewells), which was also theirs, probably from before the Conquest. In Beaconsfield they had a farm at Old Fields, between the Amersham Road and Seer Green, and another in Holm End. In 1243, Richard son of John de Stonehall received from the king a grant of free warren in his lands at Beaconsfield, an extremely rare if not unique instance of such a grant being made to a simple farmer. In those days the Stonehalls probably farmed in Chalfont as well, but by the sixteenth century they had ceased to do so, and Stonewells with its half hide of land was leased. In 1522, John Stonall was farming one of the Beaconsfield farms and his son John the other.

During a century and a half following the death of Sir John Butler in 1477, Beaconsfield had no resident squire. His eldest son was dead, and the heir was his grandson. The formal lordship, however, still resided in the abbess of Burnham until the Dissolution, though the lands that remained in her hands were a small part of the parish, the principal item being the Crown. No doubt she still held courts, which must now have derived greater authority and importance from their being no longer overtowered by the figure of the principal land-owner, though the Bulstrodes and the Wallers, who successively held leases of the Butler manor and demesnes, were formidable men.

Robert Bulstrode and Sir William his son were of ancient, and very possibly of Saxon descent, and they were connected by recent marriages with the Brudenells and the Drurys. Sir William's interests were widespread, and his appointments included offices of state, as well as that of steward to the bishop of Lincoln at Wooburn, with responsibility for the palace there, to which the bishop frequently came. He gradually acquired the three inns in the Butler fee: the Saracen's Head and the George (which he renamed the Bull in allusion to his well-known family legend) were let, and he himself resided in the King's Head. He does not appear to have been interested in the Crown.

Sir William died in 1527, leaving no children, and his wife four years later. His interests were all acquired by Robert Waller, who had previously been closely associated with him. The first Waller known to have come to this county was Richard, who in the mid-fifteenth century married a daughter of Edmund Brudenell, lord of Chalfont St Peter, of Raans in Amersham, and of other lands, and a prominent figure in local affairs. The Brudenells were a legal family, in an age when legal families were especially coherent and tightly knit. Robert, a son of Edmund Brudenell by a second marriage, pursued a successful career that ended on the Bench as Chief Justice of the Common Pleas. The names of Edmund and Robert passed into the Waller family, the former becoming a cherished favourite.

There is as yet no direct proof that the John Waller who appeared here in 1472 was Richard's son, but the fact need not be doubted. His social position, connected as he was with the Brudenells, the Bulstrodes and the Drurys, was highly satisfactory. He probably practised here as a lawyer, and as the bailiff of the abbess of Burnham. His two sons, Robert and John followed him. These two were evidently shrewd enough to foresee what lay ahead for the religious houses, and here and there in the neighbourhood they acquired small properties, at first on leasehold and then, when the catastrophe came, bidding for them as sitting tenants.

Robert Waller was twice married; in his will, which he wrote, as did Sir William

Bulstrode, with his own hand, he provided for seven sons, three from his first and four from his second marriage, as well as six daughters, all of them married. Who his first wife was is not known; his second was a daughter of William Duncombe of Wingrave—a marriage which connected him with an upstart but thriving family, steadily advancing to importance and influence in the county. His property was divided by his will among his seven sons; none of them seems to have received a preponderant share. The four inns—the Crown, the Saracen's Head, the King's Head and the Bull (lately the George) went to four of his sons. The youngest son Edmund received what appears to have been an alehouse, a few parcels of land and the lease of a small farm. Yet it was he that became his father's successor in point of wealth and prestige. He was under age when his father died, but about ten years later he married Cicely Ball, daughter of Thomas Ball who had been associated with his father in practice. There is little doubt that Edmund carried his father's firm on, though his residence was always at Stock Place in Coleshill.

Margery, one of Robert Waller's daughters, married Robert Dawbeney, the innkeeper at the Saracen's Head, which he and his father before him had kept since John Brown retired. She had been brought up in an inn, for the King's Head was her father's place of residence and doubtless his office as well. After her husband died she continued in trade on her own account, although she had grown-up sons. This marriage serves to illustrate the high social standing of the innkeepers at that time and earlier. We have the will of John Dawbeney, Robert's father, who died in 1510, but it does not tell us who he was or where he came from. We are better informed about Robert Dawbeney's friend Nicholas Cooke, who kept the Bull.

Nicholas was a kinsman of Sir Anthony Cooke of Giddy Hall in Essex; perhaps he and Sir Anthony's father were first cousins. Sir Anthony was one of those who in Mary's reign went into exile for their faith, and like others of the Marian exiles he enjoyed high prestige under Elizabeth, and spoke with authority in her parliaments. But what lent him even greater distinction was the possession of five accomplished and learned daughters (he himself had been the master of Edward VI), all of whom were married to husbands of birth and position. One was the wife of Sir William Cecil, another of Sir Nicholas Bacon; it was at the request of 'my especial good Lady Bacon' that Nicholas made a handsome bequest to his cousin Tristram Cooke 'for the virtuous bringing up of his children and their advancement'. He died a wealthy man, leaving no children of his own, and after providing for his wife and her three daughters by a former marriage, he destined the residue for friends, relatives and charitable purposes. It is the voice of a generous and kindly man that comes across to us as we read his will: one by one there come into his mind the various assets he could dispose of—a lease of Old Fields, a lease of a large farm in Farnham Royal, ready money, debts owing to him, great stocks of firewood, and the very clothes off his back; as he passed them in review, so there came into his mind those who might fittingly benefit from each. It was a lengthy will that resulted, drawn up by Robert Lee, brother to Sir Anthony Lee of Quarrendon, who had lately come to live at Gregories, and had taken to wife a daughter of Robert Dawbeney.

From a return made to the Privy Council in 1577 we have the names of three innkeepers, one taverner (Margery Dawbeney at the Saracen's Head), and twelve alehousekeepers, though none of their houses is named. The succession of the innkeepers can be more or less established through the preceding hundred years; not quite however, for the inns are seldom alluded to by their names, and these indeed sometimes changed. Nor was it usual in documents to mention the purpose for which a building was used: a house was a house, whether it was an inn, a farm or an office. John Dawbeney, for example, in 1510, bequeathed the Saracen's Head describing it as 'my mansion next the Crown', and the George as 'my mansion in Holme End'. The alehouses, for similar reasons, present even greater difficulties than the inns.

It would be a pity to leave this subject without a word about Robert Idle, who in 1577 was keeping one of the alehouses, but afterwards obtained the Saracen's Head. From the number of wills in which testators of all degrees made bequests to him, or named him as executor or overseer, it must be inferred that he was popular, capable and respected. He died an old man in 1624, leaving a wife to carry on the business, which he destined, after her death, for his cousin, another Robert Idle; she, however, must have viewed this disposition with disfavour, for she took no steps to prove the will, and being visited by two lawyers accompanied by George Grimsdale and John Newington the churchwardens to find out her intentions, 'she directly answered that she would not prove the will nor administer'. The Saracen's Head continued in the Idle family until 1714, when it was sold to Richard Rutt of the King's Head.

The most prosperous men in the town throughout the whole of this and the Stuart period were the lawyers. The leading figures in the Tudor age were John Waller (d.1498), Sir William Bulstrode (d.1527), Robert Waller (d.1545) and his brother John (d.1521), Thomas Balle (d.1559), Robert Lee (d.1572), Edmund Waller (d.1603), Richard Tredway (d.1604) and Richard Gosnold (d.1621). A large number of others can be traced who were engaged with them in the practice; many of them 'followed the Common Pleas', that is to say that they had been bred to the law, either at an Inn of Court or as apprentices. Others, however, especially in the early sixteenth century, were not lawyers but men of affairs, who had a working knowledge of figures and how to carry on a farm or a trade. They described themselves as yeomen, and some of them, like the Garstones, belonged to old local families. Their practical experience was invaluable when they acted as executors or trustees. It was in the hands of John Hawdwynne, one of these men, but sometimes described as a tailor, that John Gardiner left his building work at the King's Head. Innkeepers, too, were often associated with the lawyers, mainly but not inevitably 'on the sales side'.

The practice must have been lucrative and widely known: men came from far afield to be associated in it; members of the Petty family came from Tetsworth, George Calfield was also an Oxfordshire man, and Richard Gosnold was a member of a family practising in Suffolk—he came into the firm in the traditional way by marrying his predecessor's daughter. What the arrangements were at any time between these men it is not possible to say; one can only be sure when one sees the same men dealing side by side with other people's affairs time and time again, that there must have existed something that can properly be called a firm.

The patronage of the church until the 1520s resided in the Scudamores, descendants of the Hodengs of the thirteenth century. An advowson was commonly regarded purely as a piece of property to be exploited to the best advantage. The presentation to a vacant benefice could not be sold without committing the heinous sin of simony; but if it were not vacant there was no bar to the sale of the right of presentation expectant on the death of the then incumbent, and this is what the patron did unless he had a relative or friend on whom he wished to bestow it.

The rector might or might not reside; if he did not, he appointed and paid a curate to carry out his duties. Up to the Reformation there were also other clergy living in the parish, who were engaged in celebrating in chantries or offering prayers for deceased parishioners;

some of them probably kept little schools or did duty as tutors in the households of the well-to-do, and helped the lawyers with Latin instruments. Further, a rector who did not reside, and sometimes one who did, let the rectory and farmed out the tithes for a specified yearly sum; there was a regular market in tithes and bidders would always come forward to ensure the rector of a fair price. Some time in the 1520s, Laurence Handford, whose family had London connexions, took these tithes at farm of the rector, William Delabere, who apparently resided here until he came into an estate in Herefordshire. Laurence then settled down in the town, and two of his sisters found husbands in the neighbourhood: one of them married Thomas Reading of Chalfont St Giles, and the other became the wife of Nicholas Cooke at the Bull. In due course he purchased the advowson.

It is not until the early fifteenth century that we know anything about the church itself. As to the church that stood here in 1200, there is no saying whether it was built of stone or of timber with wattle and daub. From 1415 onwards, however, scraps of information begin to turn up. Gregory Ballard, great-grandson of old Richard Gregory and heir to Gregories, the Grove and all the Gregory lands, left instructions that his executors should completely repair the chapel of the Holy Trinity at the expense of his estate; this must have been the Trinity aisle that Sir William Bulstrode left £20 for the repair of in 1527. By then, however, the second aisle, St Anne's aisle, had been added, for that was where Sir William desired to be buried. By 1420 the church had bells, and presumably a tower, for in that year the bailiff, on the lord's instructions, made a handsome contribution towards their upkeep out of the income of the manor. When John Waller died in 1521, he left 20s towards the building of the steeple, which need mean no more than that the tower was being heightened or strengthened, probably to accommodate more, or heavier bells. It looks as if the course of this operation was halted at the Reformation and for some years afterwards, for in 1545 Robert Waller left a further 20s towards the finishing of the work, only to be paid when the workmen had begun on it.

The arms of the Butlers.

John Dabney's will. (County Record Office)

37

ABOVE: Balon's will (County Record Office), and BELOW: Capel's
House hard by Beaconsfield churchyard.

ABOVE: Saxton's 16th century map of the district (BCM) and
BELOW: The Old Rectory. (D. R. Fletcher)

39

Tudor builders left their impr
Swan; BELOW LEFT: 42/44 L
lane and BELOW CE

ABOVE CEN

BELOW

40

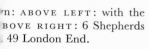

n: ABOVE LEFT: with the
BOVE RIGHT: 6 Shepherds
49 London End.

lls Farm.

Farm.

41

Wall paintings at 1 London End—ABOVE: the painted room; LEFT: lute player and RIGHT: falconer, all c1600.

The Civil War

Towards the end of the Tudor period the face of Beaconsfield began to undergo a notable change, which gathered momentum after the turn of the century. The introduction of brick to replace wattle and daub in the walls of buildings also permitted more slender framing, at a time when timber was becoming scarcer and dearer. In these circumstances landlords, for whom in general this was a time of prosperity, often found it a better proposition to re-build rather than repair their cottages and house properties. Sometimes houses were re-fronted in brick, so that their appearance was transformed and their age disguised, as at Seelys. Thus many of the buildings that we see today in the old town do not differ radically in appearance from what they were in the reign of James I. This activity was reflected in the prosperity of those who carried on the trade of building in brick, here and in the neighbour-hood. The Cock family, for instance, was in that business here and in Chalfont St Giles, and in 1648 Ralf Cock had done well enough to enable him to invest in a farm in Hughenden, and others of that family rose in the world. The will of Richard Simpson, bricklayer, who died here in 1639, shows him to have been buying small properties in the town.

The fabric of the church, on the other hand, deteriorated: people had been encouraged to acts of vandalism, and the destruction had been appalling. Most of the immense quantity of works of mediaeval art that decorated the churches and uplifted those who frequented them had been senselessly and brutally smashed—to the extent that the very fabrics of the churches suffered, for the stained glass windows were shattered, and the weather let in upon the interior. In 1634, when the churches were visited with a view to their restoration and better upkeep, the church of Beaconsfield was on the whole in rather a better state than most of those in the county, yet the chancel was reported in a shocking state, with a defective roof and the entire east wall infested with ivy and in general decay; repairs elsewhere were overdue and the bellows of the organ had been dismantled. The interior seems to have been as it were developed: wealthy parishioners had erected structures in which they sat, and other structures in which their wives and daughters sat, for in those days the men sat apart from the women; some of these erections had been reared up in the chancel itself.

The first Edmund Waller died at Stock Place, and was buried in Amersham Church in March 1603. He left three sons and seven daughters, and we can gain some idea of how wealthy he was from the fact that he bequeathed to Margaret, his only unmarried daughter the princely legacy of £1000. His son Robert succeeded him; he had been admitted to the Inner Temple in 1580, but it is doubtful whether he was ever in regular practice. His marriage to Anne, the youngest daughter of Griffith Hampden marked the apogee of the Waller fortunes, for it brought them into the orbit of the oldest and most respected family in the county. It did not at the time seem so important as it became later on that William, Griffith Hampden's son and heir, married an aunt of Oliver Cromwell.

Edmund Waller the poet was born in 1606. At some time, Robert Waller removed from

43

Coleshill to Beaconsfield—he perhaps took a lease of the manor, so the poet may have been brought up here, not at Hall Barn, for there is no evidence of a great house there at this time, but perhaps at Hall Place. Robert Waller died in 1617, evidently a stern puritan; his will opens with a commendation of prodigious length and of the hugest piety, after which it directs that his body is to be buried among the poor, deeper than usual. His children were to be brought up by their mother 'according to my degree, in virtue, learning and good manners'.

The Butlers had sold their Beaconsfield estate in the mid-sixteenth century to Lord Williams of Thame, whose daughter carried it in marriage into the Wenman family; they did not reside here, but let it, as the Butlers had done, from time to time. Robert Waller was active in the estate market; he bought Segraves, for example, and the manor of Little Kimble, and sold again when it suited him. If he in fact took a lease of this manor, he put himself in the best position to weigh up its value and its capacity for improvement, and to watch for the most favourable moment to treat for it; that moment did not come, apparently, in his lifetime, for the purchase was only carried through seven years after his death by Mistress Anne Waller on her son Edmund's behalf.

The Stuart period was a brilliant one for the Beaconsfield lawyers. Richard Tredway outlived the old queen; he had been a man of distinction, a bencher of the Inner Temple and the holder of various Crown offices. The Gosnolds, one after another, were great figures in the town and outside, and finally Thomas Smith, whose father had come into the firm as the husband of Maximilian Petty's daughter, married George Gosnold's daughter and became his worthy successor. George was the most outstanding figure; he was the third son but the eventual heir of Richard Gosnold, and he carried on the practice for more than forty years. He had important clients: he did all the Pakingtons' business in this county, and supervised their Aylesbury estate; during the Interregnum he took the forfeited lands of Robert Dormer and Francis Handford on lease, and kept them warm till his clients could repossess them. It was of course true that he was the steward of the manor of Beaconsfield, and presided in person at its courts, but he also rode out for a similar purpose to Wendover, Peterley, Taplow and elsewhere. He owned Waddendon House and what remained of Wiggenton, he lived at Overs and farmed it, he had his office near the King's Head, yet in the midst of all these preoccupations he found time for just one more: he was our brewer—he bought the brewery and carried it on. Smith obtained stewardship of almost every local manor, but left no son; the Gosnold family also failed in its male line. By the late 1720's John Charsley was the principal member of the firm, and for 200 years his family practised here and kept the manorial courts.

Mention must also be made of Richard Baldwin, who bought Wiltons in the early years of our period, and of his descendants who continued there for a century. They were one after another members of the Inner Temple, and lawyers practising in the neighbourhood as well as in London. Baldwin families were numerous, and their genealogies are notoriously tricky; the origin of this one has not been traced.

Local society consisted almost entirely of the Waller families and their kinsmen and connexions by marriage, which included the lawyers Tredway, Gosnold and Petty. The Waller families are hard to disentangle, for the junior branches were as fervently devoted to the name of Edmund as the senior; we are liable to encounter at one time an Edmund of Hall Barn, an Edmund of Gregories and an Edmund 'of the town'. Those of Gregories appear, despite the accepted pedigree, to have been descended from John, the younger brother of the first Robert, but the rest of the tribe go back to Robert himself. We shall hear again of Nathaniel Tomkins, who married Cicely, the poet's sister, and of his pitiable end; Brian Jansen, who had been sheriff of the county, Robert Thorpe, a bencher of the Middle Temple and Oliver Clobery, a London merchant with trading connexions in the New World, were remoter kinsmen but warm friends residing here. Mr Thomas Waller of Gregories was also to some extent a Londoner: he occupied the dignified and lucrative office of Protonotary of the Common Pleas.

We have not enough information to enable us to decide whether in relation to the previous century Beaconsfield, as a farming or a trading community had gone ahead or fallen behind. If taxation returns can be accepted at their face-value, it had as a whole lost ground. In 1524 it had paid about five per cent of the tax levied on the Chiltern hundreds; when ship-money was laid upon the county, and the division of the burden carefully agreed by the whole body of the gentry, the share of Beaconsfield was just two per cent. In 1524 we paid about half as much as Amersham, about six times as much as Chalfont St Giles and three times as much as Chalfont St Peter. In 1637 we paid rather more than half Amersham's share, but precisely the same as each of the two Chalfonts.

It may be doubted whether the development of wheeled traffic that set in during the latter half of Elizabeth's reign was beneficial to the town. The old road to Oxford and the West had grave disadvantages for wheeled traffic, when compared with that which followed the Bath Road to Maidenhead Thicket and there branched off to Dorchester. Coaches were at first heavy and lumbering vehicles; if they crossed the Colne into Denham they had to pass through a long stretch of heavy soil which was often waterlogged and hardly traversable; Redhill was a steep ascent, and after a few miles there came a long and arduous descent into Wycombe, and after West Wycombe the pattern repeated itself. True it was that Hounslow Heath and Maidenhead Thicket on the other route were renowned for the robbers that infested them, but so also were Sleperesdene on the way to Beaconsfield, and Holtspur Heath on the way out of it. As early as 1352, John Payn, a Beaconsfield man well-known locally, also called John Bynethe (most probably he lived at Holtspur Bottom) was taken for the death of William the taverner of Gloucester, usually called Little Willy, but was able to satisfy the jurors that Little Willy was one of a gang of robbers who lurked at Sleperesdene killing and robbing wayfarers, and that he had robbed him, John Payn, and would have slain him had he not used his knife in self-defence. The last traveller said to have been way-laid in that place was the bishop of Llandaff in 1828.

Unemployment, widespread poverty and vagrancy were disquieting in the decades preceding the Civil War, and in the parish register we meet with people dying on their wanderings, finding, perhaps, no hospitality but that of the graveyard. These stresses combined with other causes to produce a general tension, expressing itself particularly in their religious life, which was fundamental and vital to the men of that time. We have a vivid account from Beaconsfield of a state of affairs that was common enough in this countryside.

Simon Lee, who died rector in 1631, and his predecessor Nicholas Taverner had between them spanned more than fifty years of continuous residence, and to judge from the frequency with which they were present at the execution of wills, some of which they themselves drew up, they were on friendly terms with their flock, and sensitive, no doubt, to their feelings and opinions. In 1631, however, Sir Marmaduke Dayrel of Fulmer, who had either bought this presentation or intruded himself, presented John Andrewes, who appears to have had no local connexions whatever, and was a zealous and unflinching promoter of the High Church reforms of Archbishop Laud. Poor Andrewes stepped into a colony of hornets' nests. In the Chilterns a long tradition of dissent going back into the fourteenth century made men

45

suspicious of formality in religion, and disposed them to see, not only in the archbishop's reforms but also in the presence of a Catholic queen, a danger of going back to Rome; 'no Popery' became a cry that put an end to all argument or rational thought.

The letters of John Andrewes show that in his opinion the opposition he faced stemmed from all sorts and conditions of men, indeed even from his brother clergy all over the neighbourhood. It expressed itself in misbehaviour in Church: they lay down on the benches, they stubbornly refused to kneel at prayer, they sat with their hats on (which is less surprising when we remember the leaky roofs and broken windows), they never came to Church at all except on Sundays. But even if they stayed away altogether, or however they comported themselves when they came, they were never reported by the churchwardens, whose duty it was to present to the archdeacon's court all such delinquencies. This court, which from its jurisdiction in cases of moral misbehaviour, was widely called the 'bawdy court', was so disliked that churchwardens, rather than face odium and unpopularity by making presentments to it, returned an *omnia bene*. Andrewes seems to have been at loggerheads even with his own churchwardens: the parish register was not entered up during his incumbency, although what purported to be copies of it were sent to the bishop as the law required. The necessity of repairing the churches was evident enough, and of promoting more reverence at Divine Service; yet the screw which might have been gently turned was turned too violently, and the sort of thing we are considering ensured that the Great Rebellion was not that of a clique of disgruntled gentlemen and merchants, but something much more broadly based, and deeper.

On 19 January 1642, by order of Parliament, the justices met at Beaconsfield, and the train-bands mustered there. This was the first time in our history that such an order had been made by the two houses acting on their own; though it caused general surprise it was complied with. This was not the first time, on the other hand, that train-bands had been mustered here, for John Hampden had done so, eight years before, in the churchyard, for which impropriety he had been sharply rebuked by the church authorities. It would be unwise to attach any political significance to this episode, for Hampden accepted the rebuke humbly, and undertook not to repeat his action, which a man of his mettle would hardly have done if he had been acting on principle.

During the first two years of the Civil War, the king's headquarters being at Oxford, control of this county was hotly contested, and there were always parliamentary troops quartered here. Indeed they remained here far longer than military necessity required, for the cost of the war was beyond the resources of parliament to defray, and the soldiers' pay fell into arrears. They could not be disbanded unpaid, but they could be continued in service at little cost so long as they could be billeted, and so long as their officers could commandeer victuals to feed them. Yet things came to a climax here in 1645, when Sir William Waller's cavalry mutinied at their lack of pay.

The burden that the presence of these troops imposed on the inhabitants was grievous. Horses, carts and farm animals were taken from them, as well as produce, and their pastures were occupied for grazing; men and horses were quartered on their premises. After five years they were invited to submit their claims to Parliament for the damage they had sustained, and their return survives. Item by item it sets out the losses they had individually suffered, and the sum of them all amounted to upwards of £6000. The magnitude of this figure can be appreciated when it is compared with the £17 10s which had been assessed upon them in 1640 for shipmoney, the symbol of the oppression that gallant men had laid down their lives to combat. After due scrutiny the account was allowed, and the County

46

Treasurer, Mr William Russell of Chalfont St Giles, was directed to allow it to them in abatement of future taxation.

Assessments of half a year's income were made against those who were opposed to Parliament, and the lands of those who took up arms, and of Roman Catholics, were sequestered. Francis Handford lost his property in the town for recusancy. Mr John Pepys of the Temple was taken into custody for refusing to deposit half his assessment of £400, but on his paying up £100, giving security for £100 more, and agreeing to help in getting Coke's Institutes through the press, the remaining £200 were waived. When he came to Beaconsfield to join the Gosnolds is not clear, but when parish registers were discontinued he became Registrar of the parish responsible to the magistrates for the continuance of similar records. There was trouble also at the White Hart. Thomas, son of Michael Edgerley the landlord was taken and imprisoned for carrying messages to and fro from Oxford to London, but was released on bond to give up the practice.

Robert Aldridge of Woodlands was one of those who came forward at this time, and upon whom the County Committee placed reliance. He was active from the outset in the parliamentary forces, and soon he was promoted to be a Captain of Horse. Apart from his military duties he was employed in a variety of official matters, and was appointed a magistrate. His name appears with frequency in the public records until his death in 1658.

Edmund Waller, though less than forty years old when the Civil War broke out, had fifteen years of parliamentary experience behind him, having sat for the borough of Amersham in three successive parliaments. We need not tell here the oft-told tale of 'Waller's Plot', which ignominiously ended its first half: suffice it to say that Mr Nathaniel Tomkins his fellow conspirator was hanged like a common felon, and in front of his own front-door in Holborn, while he himself paid £10,000 (as well as £1000 assessed upon him while he was lodged in the Tower) for a pardon, and leave to exile himself to France. It cannot be supposed that he had ever spent much time here, nor did he in all probability till he was an elderly man and built Hall Barn. The likelihood is that he left the management of the estate in his mother's capable hands. Two years after he went into exile, the manorial courts that Mr George Gosnold presided over were those of Mistress Anne Waller.

The poet was permitted to return in 1651, and he then took out, as it were, a single-premium insurance policy by exercising his highest powers in a panegyric on the Protector, which he renewed at the Restoration through an encomium on King Charles II. He represented Hastings in the Restoration parliament, afterwards bestowing the like honour on many places, and ending up in Cornwall. He lived on into the next reign and died in October 1687 at the age of eighty one.

His influence at Beaconsfield must have been exercised in the king's favour, as was that of the Wallers of Gregories also, for they held Court appointments. Close at hand, however, was an active and potent influence in the contrary direction. In the palace that had once been that of the bishops of Lincoln at Wooburn lived Philip Lord Wharton, who received and entertained there dissenters from all over the neighbourhood. His son Thomas, an ardent and immensely successful political manager, was able to exploit the affection his father had earned.

At the same time, a sinister figure appeared on the other side of the parish; the manor of Bulstrode, which extended into Beaconsfield and included Hillmott Farm, was purchased by Lord Jeffreys of Wem, the celebrated Judge Jeffreys. No ill, however, came of it, and Sir Thomas Clayton, who bought the Vache in Chalfont St Giles after its forfeiture by George Fleetwood, was a more malevolent persecutor of Quakers and dissenters.

47

The town that we now quit, after having passed briefly in review some of the features of its story over eight hundred years, was not altogether unlike the town we know. If it was more beautiful, it was probably dirtier: more noisome things than waste paper could be seen in its streets and lanes. It was also much wetter, for it was irrigated by streams which pursued their regular courses through it. At Anne Waller's court in 1645 it was ordered:

'That Michael Edgerley (at the White Hart) shall scour and cleanse . . . the ditch in Shepherd's Lane, and the ditch lying against his own garden.

'That the watercourse that runs by the end of Shepherd's Lane shall be kept in the course wherein it now runs, through the land of Robert Aldridge, gent.

'That the watercourse that runs out of the street in Wycombe Way shall be kept in the ditch till it comes below the well, and across the Way, and so go down the ditch to Waddenton Pond.'

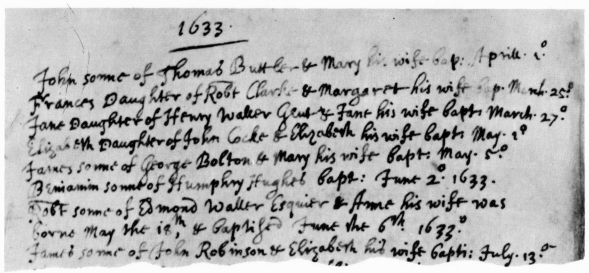

ABOVE: Thomas Waller and his wife Dorothea were commemorated in Beaconsfield Church in 1626, and BELOW: Edmund Waller's son was born in 1633, as the church registers testify. (County Record Office)

THE COPIE OF

A Later sent from the Right Honorable the

Lord *PAGET*, Lord Lieutenant of the County of BUCKINGHAM,
To the Right Honorable the Earle of Holland : Shewing the great
readinesse of that County, to obey the Ordinance of the
Parliament, touching the MILITIA.

My Lord,

Have received so great expressions from my Countrymen of
Buckingham-shire, of their good affections to the Publique,
and ready Obedience to the Commands of Parliament, in the
present Muster this day begun for a fourth part of this County,
that I held it my duty to make your Lordship acquainted therewith, to the end an account may be given of it to the Parliament, if your Lordship
shall think fit.

Ten of my Deputy Lieutenants met me this morning at *Beckonsfield*, where we
called over the Traine Band, consisting but of one hundred and fifty men, who
made a very good appearance with their Armes and supplies, and as full as they
have been formerly upon any other summons. Besides these, eight score Voluntiers
and upwards within this Division, presented themselves to us very well armed, and
exercised in two Companies ; more in number then the Trained Band, summoned
to this place. I am also informed of another Company of an hundred and fifty Voluntiers more within this Division, that intend to shew themselves in our way to the
next place of meeting, and of another Company of an hundred more, who there
intend to meet us, besides the Trained Band.

This publique testimony of my Countrymens good affections, for the safety of
the King and Kingdome, I thought not unfit to make knowne. And rest

Beckonsfield 23.
May. 1642.

Your Lo⁺ *most dutifull son,*
and humble servant,

WILL: PAGET.

LONDON, Printed for JOHN BULL, dwelling in Grub-street. 1642.

LEFT: Near neighbour John Hampden helped to start
the Civil War. (Margaret Sale)

RIGHT: William Waller commanded locally, (Mansell Collection), and
Lord Paget reported that 150 men assembled at
Beckonsfield. (Lord Burnham)

ABOVE: Lord Wharton built Wooburn House, where the Bishop's Palace once stood. (BCM)

BELOW: Hyde Farm, Beaconsfield.

50

ABOVE: The Royal White Hart—without the hart. (D. R. Fletcher)

BELOW: 17th century Beaconsfield trade tokens—two of these bear the names Thomas Cocke and John Foscet. (BCM)

LEFT: The old brewery, now The Malt House; RIGHT: Jordans Meeting
House in 1798, (BCM), and BELOW: Two Gosnold
signatures of 1660. (BCM)

THE

HISTORY

OF THE

LIFE

OF

Thomas Ellwood.

Or, an Account of his BIRTH,
EDUCATION, &c.

WITH

Divers Obfervations on his Life and Manners
when a Youth: And how he came to be
Convinced of the *Truth*; with his many
Sufferings and Services for the fame.

Alfo Several Other
Remarkable Paffages and *Occurrences*.

Written by his own hand.

To which is added, A

SUPPLEMENT

By J. W.

Heb. 11. 2. *By Faith the Elders obtained a good Report.*

The Second Edition.

London : Printed and Sold by the Affigns of *J. Sowle,*
in *White-Hart-Court* in *Gracious-Street,* 1714.

Thomas Ellwood's life story, in this version of 1714
and his home at Hunger Hill. (Both BCM)

Edmund Waller, (Dr G. Wyatt), his arms, and the
Waller home at Stock Place, Coleshill.

54

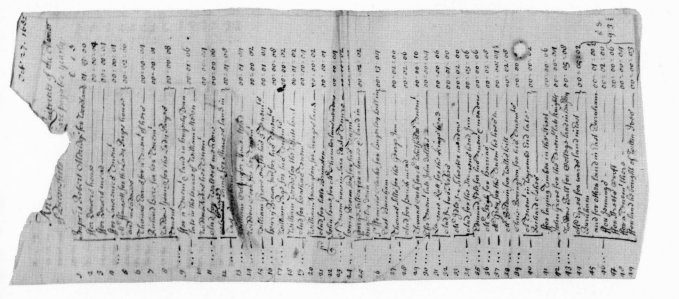

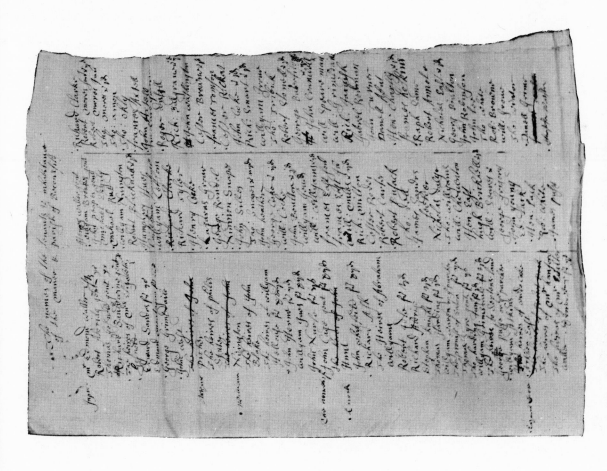

LEFT: People who lived in the manor and parish of Beconsfield in 1630 and
RIGHT: The 1682 quit rent roll. (County Record Office)

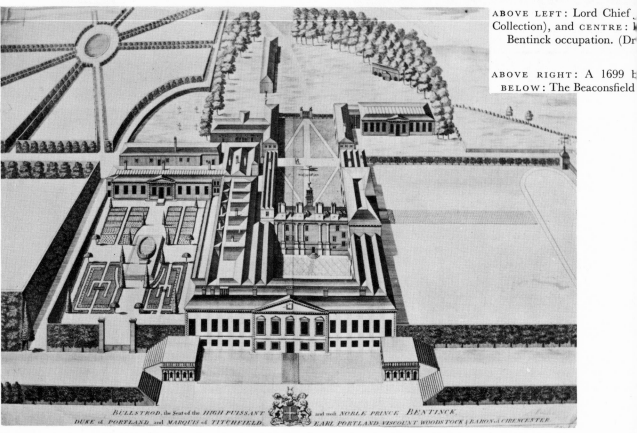

BULLSTROD, the Seat of the *HIGH PUISSANT* and most *NOBLE PRINCE BENTINCK.*
DUKE of *PORTLAND* and *MARQUIS* of *TITCHFIELD.* *EARL PORTLAND VISCOUNT WOODSTOCK & BARON of CIRENCESTER*

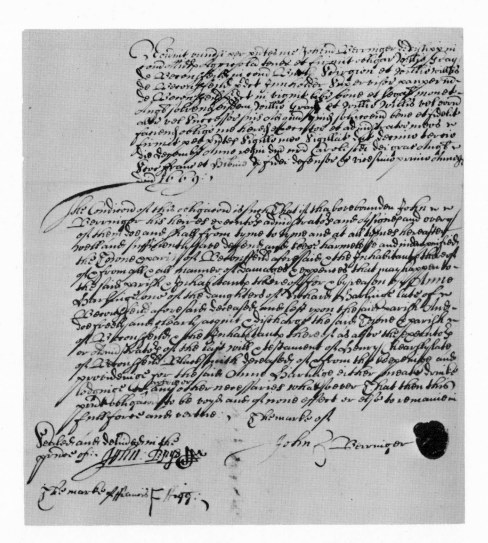

ge Jeffreys in 1684, (Mansell
Bulstrode in later years under
BELOW: a bird's eye view
)

ing Beaconsfield parish, and
b of Dame Ann Hyde, who

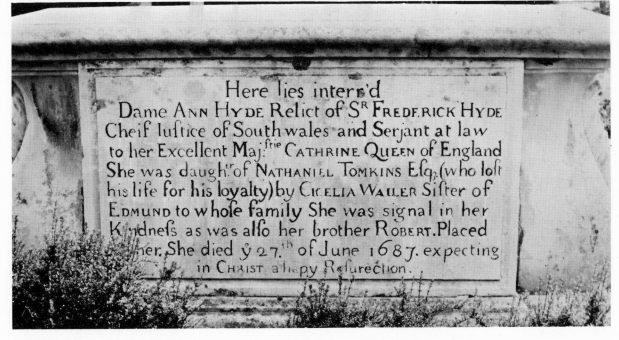

Here lies interr'd
Dame ANN HYDE Relict of SR FREDERICK HYDE
Cheif Iustice of South wales and Serjant at law
to her Excellent Maj:stie CATHRINE QUEEN of England
She was daught:r of NATHANIEL TOMKINS Esq:₃ (who loft
his life for his loyalty) by CICELIA WALLER Sifter of
EDMUND to whofe family She was signal in her
Kindnefs as was alfo her brother ROBERT. Placed
her. She died ÿ 27th of June 1687. expecting
in CHRIST a happy Refurection.

ABOVE: Beaconsfield Church, with Waller's tomb on the left, and BELOW: with the Rectory House in architect Buckler's sketch. (British Library)

ABOVE: the King's Head, no longer an inn and
BELOW: The George.

LEFT: Edmund Waller from the painting at Hall Barn; RIGHT: the original house in an early sketch, (both Lord Burnham), and BELOW: Woollcott's drawing of the grounds at Hall Barn, *c*1800. (Dr G. Wyatt)

Hall Barn

The estate that became Beaconsfield Manor was originally part of the Manor of Burnham. At Domesday the tenancy was held by Walter Fitz Otho, whose family, the Windsors, held it until the 13th century. Richard, Earl of Cornwall, granted it to Burnham Abbey in 1265. Hall, Halland or Hall Barn Manor was held in the 15th century of Burnham Abbey. In 1546 Sir John Williams was lord of Hall Barn Manor and joined it to Beaconsfield.

The Manor passed through various hands until the Wenmans emerged as principal holders, and in 1624 Anne Waller and her son Edmund acquired it. The Wallers were no strangers to the town, their forbears having recorded associations as far back as the 14th century, and in 1472 John Waller had witnessed a charter at Beaconsfield, while his son Robert became bailiff for Burnham Abbey. Of Robert's thirteen children, the youngest, Edmund, leased Little Dernedene Farm; Edmund's son, Robert owned Holloways Farm and the Bull, and it was his widow who bought Hall Barn Manor.

Two hundred years later the Wallers sold up to Sir Gore Ouseley, whose son the Rev Sir Frederick sold it in turn in 1846 to John Hargreaves, who was by then living in Waller's house. In 1870 Allan Morrison bought it, and he sold it to Sir Edward Levy-Lawson, later Lord Burnham. The Burnhams still own and occupy the Manor and the house.

If Waller dominates Beaconsfield's story, Hall Barn dominates the modern landscape, with its immaculate avenues and garden and its well managed modern farmlands. Waller is believed to have been largely responsible for the design of the house and the grounds.

Waller the poet rather than Waller the man of affairs conceived the house, much as we know it today, though additions and demolitions have intervened on a grand scale. He is thought to have built it after his return from exile, most say in 1675, though one school of thought has it that he did so somewhat earlier, after he laid out the grounds in the 1650s. But there is no record to prove either date.

The original house was rectangular, three storeys high on a north-south axis. In 1730 Edmund's son Henry added a single wing to the north-west, connected to the house by a curving wall. Effectively, the new wing housed stables and servants in two storeys. A century later, Gore Ouseley added a new southern front, extending the length of the building. The new apartments included a library fit for royal reception, in this case of Queen Adelaide. Ouseley also probably moved the staircase. Some of Waller's original rooms disappeared in the process.

When the Burnhams acquired house and estate, Sir Edward Lawson built the ballroom in 1885, restoring the symmetry of the house; one of the products of the various extensions was to put the kitchen sixty yards from the dining room, and down several steps.

Lord and Lady Burnham in 1963 found themselves faced with a somewhat intractable problem—how to economically let or occupy a house both too large for modern conditions and upkeep, and too inefficient to improve without major surgery. The Burnhams decided to eliminate their own forbear's and Ouseley's additions, remodel inside where necessary, install modern systems and recreate the best of the original decor.

In 1969 work commenced, and by May 1972 Hall Barn emerged smaller, simpler, more adapted to modern life—and much as Waller knew it, from the outside at least, though with numerous internal differences. His portrait still hangs in the house, never having left it since he put it there. It has since been joined by that of Lucy, his namesake's and Gregories kinsman Edmund's wife—painted by Kneller. Once again Hall Barn is a home, and many regard it as more handsome than before its reduction. With modern refacing and structural work, it is also more sound, and will doubtless stand as a monument to Waller and the Burnhams for another three centuries, one of the few surviving examples of a Commonwealth country home.

Hall Barn is framed by Waller's grounds. These derive inspiration from his exile and from Versailles—perhaps the first formal reflection of the French mode in this country. Interestingly, many commentators have remarked the lack of relationship between house and garden, perhaps brought about by their separate development, for the grounds were virtually certainly laid out first. Waller's view of landscape was romantic rather than picturesque, his most impressive gift to posterity, the Grove. This was laid out in straight walks, punctuated by statuary and follies. One obelisk carries both the Waller arms, and sculpted garden tools, possibly those of George II's royal gardener, Charles Bridgeman, who is believed to have tended the grounds and who may have had a hand in their final layout.

Today the M40 divides the estate, but a modern bridge links the town and its premier house, maintaining that proper distinction between community and manor.

Lucy Waller of Gregories, from the Kneller painting
at Hall Barn. (Lord Burnham)

ABOVE: Another of Woollcott's drawings showing the 1724 Garden Room
(Dr G. Wyatt), and BELOW: Colin Campbell's original
design. (Lord Burnham)

63

ABOVE LEFT: Aesculapius, an ancient Grecian statue in the grounds, and
RIGHT: the famed Temple of Venus.

BELOW LEFT: The Garden Room as it is today, and RIGHT: the Obelisk.

ABOVE LEFT: Sir Gore Ouseley, (Mansell Collection), and RIGHT: the house with his additions (BCM), and the Ouseley arms.

BELOW: The view from the lake as Ouseley would have seen it. (BCM)

65

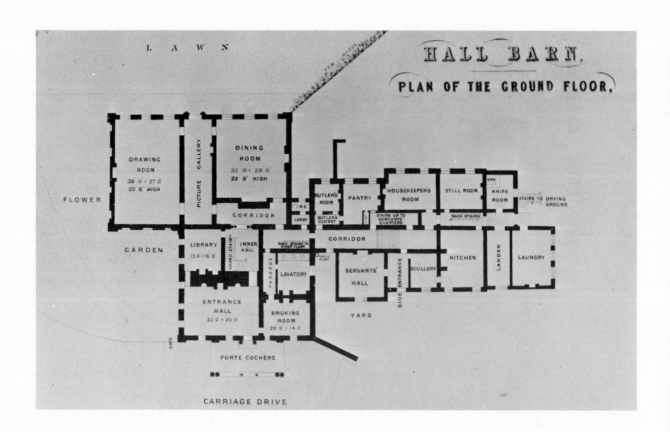

ABOVE: The 1880 plan of the ground floor, and BELOW: an earlier 1847
scheme for 'beautifying' the house that happily never
happened. (Both Lord Burnham)

BUCKINGHAMSHIRE.

IN THE MOST POPULAR DISTRICT IN THE ROYAL COUNTIES.

PARTICULARS

OF A HIGHLY VALUABLE AND ENJOYABLE RESIDENTIAL AND

Freehold Sporting Domain,

Situate adjoining the TOWN OF BEACONSFIELD, Eight Miles from Slough and Seven Miles from the Taplow Stations, on the Main Line, and Two Miles and a Half from Wooburn Green Station on the Wycombe Branch of the Great Western Railway, and Twenty-two Miles from London, and known as the

HALL BARN ESTATE,

And Comprising a Commodious and Extremely

COMFORTABLE MANSION,

In excellent order and repair, having been thoroughly decorated and restored by the late Owner, since he purchased the Estate Six Years ago.

It is remarkably well built, is approached by Carriage Drive through the Park, and entered by a Porte Cochère.

It contains a choice

Suite of Handsome Reception Rooms,

They having been built for the purpose of entertaining King William IV and Queen Adelaide; and all necessary Bed Rooms, Servants' Apartments, Kitchens and other Offices, and Excellent Cellars.

THE STABLE AND COACH HOUSE PREMISES

Were built about Three Years ago according to Plans specially prepared for the late Owner, and are all that could be desired.

THE GARDENS AND PLEASURE GROUNDS

Are of an unusually attractive character, and

THE GRANDLY-TIMBERED PARK

Embraces an area of about 400 Acres. There are about

FIFTEEN USEFUL FARMS,

Nearly all the Houses and Homesteads are conveniently arranged, well built, and in excellent order and repair.

THE WOODS, PLANTATIONS, AND SHOOTING GROUNDS,

Contain about 620 ACRES, and are admirably dispersed over the Estate for the preservation of Game, and afford some of the best Sporting in the District.

The whole comprises an Area of about

3,207 ACRES,

WHICH, WITH THE MANOR OF BEACONSFIELD,

Will be Sold by Auction,

In consequence of the decease of the late proprietor, ALLAN MORRISON, Esq., by

MESSRS. DRIVER & CO.,

AT THE MART, TOKENHOUSE YARD, LOTHBURY, LONDON,

On TUESDAY, the 20th day of JULY, 1880,

At TWO O'CLOCK precisely, in ONE LOT, unless an acceptable offer by Private Contract be previously made.

Particulars, with Plans and Views, may be had at the Swan and Crispin Inns, Burnham Village; the Crown Inn, Burnham Common; the Crown Hotel, Slough; the Saracen's Head, Beaconsfield; the Bear Hotel, Maidenhead; Skindle's Hotel, at Maidenhead Bridge; the White Hart, Windsor; the Randolph, Oxford; the Great Western Hotel, Birmingham; the Bell, Gloucester; at the Auction Mart and Estate Exchange, Tokenhouse Yard, Lothbury; of Messrs. ASHURST, MORRIS, CRISP, & CO., Solicitors, 6, Old Jewry, E.C.; of Messrs. RAWLENCE & SQUAREY, Surveyors and Land Agents, Salisbury, and 22, Great George Street, Westminster; and of Messrs. DRIVER & CO. Surveyors, Land Agents, and Auctioneers, 4, Whitehall, London.

ABOVE LEFT: The Levy-Lawson arms, and BELOW: an aerial view of the house after the ballroom was added, (D. R. Fletcher), while RIGHT: this was the sale document of 1880. (BCM)

67

ABOVE: The completed house in the 19th century, (Lord Burnham) and
BELOW: the ballroom. (National Monument Records)

HALL BARN
1972

ABOVE: A modern sketch of the house virtually restored to its original
shape by Bird & Tyler Associates of Chenies, (Lord Burnham),
and BELOW: in 1976.

69

ABOVE: Behind the scenes at Hall Barn today, and
BELOW: the Lodge.

70

ABOVE LEFT: Hall Barn, showing the curved room, and RIGHT: the old pound, now the Hall Barn Estate Office in Aylesbury End. BELOW: The view from Hall Barn's bridge over the M40.

On the Freindshipp betwixt Zacharissa and Amorett

Tell mee lovely loving Payre
why soe kinde, and soe severe
why soe carelefs of our Care
Onely to yo: Selves soe deare.

By this running change off heards
you the power of Love controule
While the Boyes deluded Darts
Can arrive att neither Soule.

ABOVE LEFT: Waller's eternal gaze meets the lively eyes of RIGHT: his Sacharissa, sculpted by Rysbrake, (Lord Burnham and BCM); while BELOW: Waller penned these lines for her.

Go, Lovely Rose!

Edmund Waller was born on 3 March 1606 at Stock Place in Coleshill. The family originated from Speldhurst, Kent, where Richard Waller had taken Charles Duke of Orleans as a prisoner from the battle of Agincourt in 1415. Part of the Waller coat of arms dates from this time when Henry V granted, in addition to his own arms, that of Orleans, hanging by a label on an oak or walnut tree, the three golden lilies hanging over a hog which runs beneath the tree and the motto 'Here is the fruit of virtue'.

Though intelligent, Edmund's education was somewhat marred 'by several ill, dull and ignorant schoolmasters till he went to Mr Dobson at Wickham' (Aubrey). From there he was sent to Eton and later to King's College, Cambridge. He became a member of Parliament for Amersham at 16 years of age but it is not likely that this was anything other than a formal appointment. With his mother, Ann, who came from the Hampden family, he bought the manors of Hall Barn and Gregories and came to live there. It is not clear in which house he lived, but it does seem likely from what Edmund Burke said of the poet living not 100 yards from his house that it was the house now known as Gregories Farm. Here his time was spent in study and country pursuits and it was here that some of his early verse was written, for in 1625 he wrote poems congratulating the King on the improvement of his fleet, on the defeat of the pirates on the Barbary Coast and on the Restoration of St Paul's Cathedral.

In 1632 he married Anne Banks a wealthy heiress from Worcestershire at St Margaret's Westminster, but she died two years later and was buried at Beaconsfield, leaving a son, Robert, who died a juvenile and a daughter. It is at this time that Thomas Hobbes who came to be tutor to Robert and George Morley (later Bishop of Winchester) joined the household. The latter was a member of the Literary Club and frequent visitors to Beaconsfield were Lucius Cary (Lord Falkland) d. 1643, and Bishop Chillingworth (1602-44). In 1642 the young widower married a second time, Mary Bressy of Thame who bore four sons and six daughters. What sort of a man was Waller? Physically he was of medium height, dark complexion with prominent eyes. He was a convivial companion and though he drank only water it is said that the fertility of his mind enlightened any gathering and Mr Saville said that 'no man in England should keep him company without drinking but Ned Waller'.

His second marriage brought to an end the series of poems written for several ladies of high birth which included 'Go lovely rose' for Lady Dorothea Sidney, but his reputation as a poet was well established, Denham in 'Coopers Hill' referring to him as 'the best of poets'.

Waller has been much criticised for alleged changes in political attitudes, but we must remember the difficulties of the times and dwell rather on his great respect for the privileges of Parliament and his attempt also to be loyal to Charles I. In 1640 he warned Charles that 'there is nothing more hard than to impose religion on free men' and in July 1641 he exposed the dangerous consequences of saying that Parliament had no right to interfere with the levying of Ship Money. It is said that his speech on the latter sold 20,000 copies in a day. His eloquence in the House was said to exceed that of Addison and Prior. In early November of the same year Waller with Falkland and Hyde, were among those who voted against the Grand Remonstrance to the King, being convinced that reform had gone far enough.

On the 22 August 1642 he espoused the cause of Charles at Nottingham by sending him one thousand gold pieces but by the following year it was not quite so clear whether Waller sided with King or Parliament. Then MP for St Ives, Cornwall, Waller was not sure that Pym genuinely wanted peace and Waller had put out feelers among the London Royalists to determine their numbers and strength with the hope that London might be regained for the King and the war ended. The result was that Waller was arrested on 31 May and required to plead his case before the Commons. They were not satisfied with his pleas. He was condemned to death but reprieved by the Earl of Essex, and he was expelled to serve a prison sentence for a year, fined £10,000, before being banished from the Kingdom. It is said that his life was saved by bribes and that some of the family property in Beaconsfield was sold for this purpose, but the sentence was revoked in 1651 which enabled Waller to return to Hall Barn in 1654.

1655 saw him appointed Commissioner for Trade and this was the year of his panegyric to Protector Cromwell. Upon the Restoration of Charles II Waller rejoiced 'Upon His Majesties Happy return'. When Charles compared the latter unfavourably with the Protector's panegyric the poet replied 'we poets always succeed better in composing fiction than in adorning truth'. In Charles' First Parliament Waller served on the Councils of Trade and Foreign Plantations. This was no sinecure; he worked hard at his job attending meetings regularly and helping draft reports and instructions as part of the Council's day to day business. As an old man, Burnet tells us, his wit entranced the House of Commons, for he said the liveliest things of any among them.

His poetry continued and his critical faculties were unusual for the time. He once described to the Duke of Buckingham Milton's 'Paradise Lost' as distinguished only by its length. Waller's reputation as a poet suffered a decline in the nineteenth century, but recent studies have placed him in historical perspective. His poetry was widely read between 1630 and 1740. In 1691 Dryden wrote of Waller 'I am desirous of laying hold on his memory on all occasions and thereby acknowledging to the world that unless he had written, none of us could write'. The inscription 'who among the poets of the age was universally acknowledged to be the first' on his tomb is no empty boast. Waller was a member of the Royal Society committee 'for improving the English tongue' and with others involved in an attempt to set up an English Academy after the French model. His ideals of order, sanity, and reasonableness dominated the coming century.

It is thought that he was himself responsible for the building of Hall Barn Manor in about 1675. Waller died at Hall Barn on 21 October 1687 and was buried in Beaconsfield churchyard, but Waller was not the last of Beaconsfield's poets.

George Crabbe 1754-1832 lived in Beaconsfield for only eighteen months, but as these months 'entirely, and for ever, changed the nature of his worldly fortunes' it seems right that his stay should be recorded. Born in Aldeburgh, Suffolk, his father was a collector of salt duties who apprenticed his son to a surgeon at the age of fourteen. After this, in London George walked the hospitals for a year but returned to Aldeburgh to practise a profession in which he had little interest.

In 1779 he set off for London again to try to make his mark on literary circles. But the few poems he had written, a box of clothes, a case of surgical instruments and three pounds brought him nothing but poverty. On the day he wrote to Burke he was 'an outcast, without friends, without employment, without bread' but within twenty-four hours he had not only found a patron but one who took him to his own house, criticised his poems mercilessly, found him publishers for 'The Library' and 'The Village', and turned him from a country boy to a man who mixed with society at all levels.

As we read the lines of 'The Library' can we envisage the Library at Gregories with Burke's books lining the shelves? Divinity was certainly one of Edmund Burke's interests, and his theological outlook was clearly that of one who knew the early Christological controversies and from his own personal background knew the significance of the Calvinists, Jesuits and Quakers mentioned in Crabbe's poem. We know that Burke is intended in the lines from 'The Borough' written after Crabbe left Gregories but clearly with a recognition of a debt.

> 'That pious moralist, that reasoning saint!
> Can I of worth like thine, Eusebius speake?
> The man is willing but the muse is weak.'

Crabbe returned to Aldeburgh having taken Holy Orders and was able to marry Sarah Elmy in 1783 eleven years after he had first met her. While he was bringing up his family there was a silence of twenty-two years. His later years, after the death of his wife in 1813, were spent in botany and writing poetry till his death in 1832. Most of his poetry concerned the common people and the country life of his day. Benjamin Britten brought to life Peter Grimes who Crabbe must surely have known at Aldeburgh. His poetry has much to offer for a *real* understanding of human nature—of the mind and of the body.

G. K. Chesterton (1874-1936) came to live in Beaconsfield in 1909 living first at Overroads until 1922. He wrote poetry from his boyhood winning the Milton Prize while at St Paul's School. This was a poem on St Francis Xavier and whilst much of what he wrote later is serious, some of the first published work was 'Greybeards at Play' which W. H. Auden described as 'some of the best pure nonsense verse in English.'

The ballade was a form which suited Chesterton's outlook on life and appeared throughout his years. Some of the earlier ones were 'A Ballade of Professional Pride', 'A Ballade of Monsters', 'A Ballade to a Philanthropist' and 'A Ballade of Great Rivers' where the Envoi declares

> Prince—is that you? Lor lumme! O Gorblime . . .
> (I too resume the speech of my degree)
> O crickey, Bill . . . Lor luvaduck!—Well I'm . . .
> Returning rivers to the ancient sea.

This vein continued throughout his life with Beaconsfield people and events. When loyalties conflicted at a cricket match between the town and a team of authors seven verses were penned to commemmorate 'My town against my trade', and the controversy over the war memorial is remembered in a poem.

But the field is much wider than this. Chesterton takes his place in the nation's history by his poetic record of some of the great events of the past. If you want to visit the Vale of the White Horse then guide books will recommend you before you go, to read 'The Ballad of the White Horse' published in 1911, to gather the events and spirit of the times in pre-Conquest England. In the ballad Chesterton tells of the defence of England by King Alfred against the heathen Danes and how Our Lady appears to Alfred in a vision and says

75

I tell you naught for your comfort
Yea naught for your desire
Save that the sky grows darker yet
And the sea rises higher.

This verse was taken up by Sir Winston Churchill in the dark days of nineteen forty and has been much quoted since.

His love for England is expressed in poem after poem.

St George he was for England,
And before he killed the dragon
He drank a pint of English ale
Out of an English flagon.
For though he fast right readily
In hair-shirt or in mail
It isn't safe to give him cakes
Unless you give him ale.

Then there is 'The Rolling English Road' made by 'the rolling English drunkard' and the attempt to straighten the road 'the night we went to Glastonbury by way of Goodwin Sands'.

The spirit of patriotism is taken up in 'The Secret People'. 'Smile at us, pay us, pass us; but do not quite forget. For we are the people of England, that never have spoken yet'; much quoted among undergraduates in the Oxford of the twenties.

But other nations are included in the Collected Poems 'Poland'. 'Me Heart' beginning 'I came from Castlepatrick . . .'; 'Lepanto' was popular when it was published during the First World War with its stirring tale of the defence of Christian Europe under Don John of Austria.

The Christian Verse includes 'The Donkey', one of the few poems remembered by heart from childhood in the present writer's generation. But there is also 'The Beatific Vision', those with a Christmas theme, and many which show the mainspring of Chesterton's thought in the Christian thesis. The hymn 'O God of earth and altar' appears in most of the hymnals and Miss Helen Gardner has placed 'Anti-Christ, or the Reunion of Christendom' to represent one of her choice of G. K. Chesterton's poems. This is a good example of the width and depth of G. K.'s writing—Christian with an immediately contemporary challenge.

Top Meadow, across the road from Overroads, began with the Studio in 1912 but it was not until 1922 that the house was added. Here G. K. died in 1936, and Walter de la Mare, a frequent visitor, gives us a fitting reminder in his tribute to Gilbert Keith Chesterton, of the poet's character and his place in this Chiltern town.

Knight of the Holy Ghost, he goes his way
Wisdom his motley, Truth his loving jest;
The mills of Satan keep his lance in play
Pity and innocence his heart at rest.

Mr. *WALLERS SPEECH,*

In the Houſe of Commons, the fourth
of *July*, 1643. being broᵤght to the Bar, and
having leave given him by the Speaker, to
ſay what he could for himſelfe.

Mr. Speaker.

I Acknowledge it a great mercy of God, and a great favour from you, that I am once more ſuffered to behold this Honourable Aſſembly, I mean not to make uſe of it to ſay any thing in my own defence by Juſtification or denyall of what I have done, I have already confeſſed enough to make me appeare, worthy not onely to be put out of this Houſe, but out of the World too. All my humble requeſt to you is, that, if I ſeeme to you as unworthy to live, as I doe to my ſelfe, I may have the Honour to receive my death from your owne hands, and not bee expoſed to a Tryall by the Counſell of Warre : what ever you ſhall thinke me worthy to ſuffer in a Parliamentary way, is not like to finde ſtop any where elſe.

ABOVE: Part of Waller's famous speech to the Commons in 1643, and
BELOW: his tomb as engraved by C. J. Smith. (Dr G. Wyatt)

ABOVE LEFT: G. K. Chesterton as he is remembered by Beaconsfield, and RIGHT: Crabbe in 1826, (Mansell Collection). BELOW: Chesterton's studio at Top Meadow.

78

ABOVE LEFT: An unusual Czech commemmorative stamp of GKC, and
RIGHT: a statuette at Top Meadow, with BELOW: Chesterton's own
cartoon of the elegiac Gray.

ABOVE & OPPOSITE ABOVE: Chesterton's Ballade of
Hampden's Cross, in his own hand.

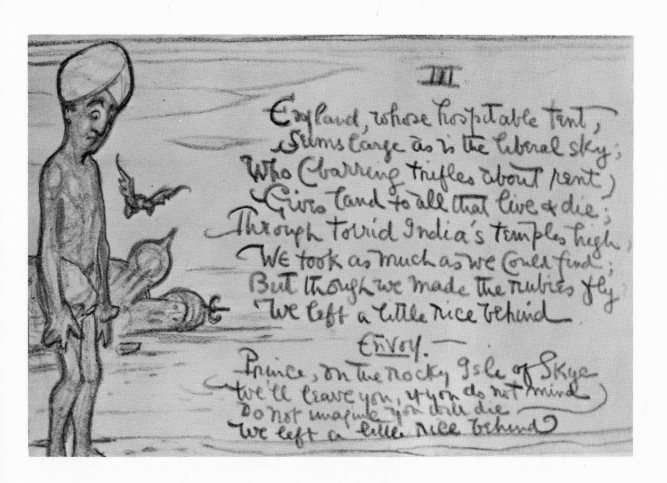

III

England, whose hospitable tent,
Seems large as is the liberal sky;
Who (barring trifles about rent)
Gives land to all that live & die;
Through torrid India's temples high,
We took as much as we could find;
But though we made the rubies fly,
We left a little rice behind —

Envoy. —

Prince, on the rocky Isle of Skye
We'll leave you, if you do not mind —
Do not imagine you will die —
We left a little rice behind

CLARE
at the LYME CARNIVAL
Riding on the Unicorn

BELOW: Another Chesterton original for Clare, one of the children who
visited him at Top Meadow. (All GKC sketches
by permission of Dorothy Collins)

Edmund Burke from Joshua Reynolds' painting, (Dr G. Wyatt), and his
'dagger'. (Lord Burnham)

Witty and Wise

The coach road from London to Oxford has brought to Beaconsfield many famous names in history and literature. Here we shall begin with the seventeenth century and the time of Edmund Waller the poet who, apart from ten years in exile, lived the greater part of his life in these folds of the Chiltern Hills. The Wallers were related to the Hampdens and the Cromwells. Edmund's mother Ann who purchased the Gregories and the Hall Barn Estates in 1624 was a staunch Royalist and on one of the Protectors visits to Hall Barn, while Edmund was in France, she reproached him with the execution of King Charles. Oliver folded his napkin and flung it in her face saying 'I'll not dispute with thee kinswoman.' After the Restoration Charles II was another visitor.

When *Edmund Burke* purchased his estate in 1768, hospitality to the great people of the day, tended to be at Gregories. Here came Sir Joshua Reynolds and Doctor Johnson, in 1774 accompanied by the Thrales on their return from the Welsh tour. David Garrick came and so did Oliver Goldsmith proclaiming his host 'too nice for a statesman, too proud for a wit'. However, despite this stricture, it is impossible to be in Beaconsfield for many hours, without being confronted with what Chesterton called its patron statesman. Burkes Road and Burkes Crescent contain the land which was the gardens and orchards surrounding the mansion house and the stables survive in Burkes Cottage. A cedar tree planted by Burke grows in Butlers Court garden. The pond near Butlers Court School was the old Stonepath Pond so-called because the remains of Burke's old mill ran across it and is at the bottom of what was Mill Lane. Several houses in the conservation area are named after him. If you want to sit on a seat which came from the mansion house go to the Royal Standard Inn at Forty Green where in the lounge there is a great ship's settle—and an open basket fireholder.

There are other Burke relics in the locality including a chair at Hughenden Manor, some china at Hall Barn and the dagger thrown on the floor of the House of Commons during one of the debates on the sale of arms to France.

It is well that we remember him. His contribution to English political thought far outweighs the ministerial positions he held, for he was never a member of the cabinet. This stemmed from that part of his character which greatly impressed strangers who perceived the way he carried out the smaller courtesies of life—the way he descended the steps at Gregories to receive guests and, in his own house or at table, how attentive he was to those of inferior rank. To beggars he was kind and charitable so that when returning home by hackney coach he had to go into the house to disburse the coachman. When cautioned about his assisting an old man thought to have been the victim of gin Burke replied 'He is an old man, and if gin be his comfort, let him have gin.'

From Michaelmas 1809 *William Hickey* (1749-1830) the memoirist leased Little Hall Barn and lived there for seven years. Most of his life was spent in India where he practised in the Supreme Court of Bengal. He was a hard worker with a passion for wine, women and gambling. 'I never could depend upon myself' he said 'when embarked on convivial society.' An adventurer, perhaps, the pages of his books stained with claret, he chronicled late eighteenth century India, and was able to see Wellesley and Cornwallis in an unconventional wav.

He had a great eye for colour as we see in a passage relating how the Earl Ferrers was hanged for killing his steward.

'His Lordship was conveyed to Tyburn in his own landau, dressed in a superbe suit of white and silver, being the clothes in which he was married; his reason for wearing which was that they had been his first step towards ruin, and should attend his exit.'

Hickey was known to the Burke family before he took the lease of Little Hall Barn and refers to 'my respected friend Mr Edmund Burke' relating also a characteristic letter written by Burke on behalf of a total stranger, recently convicted on flimsy evidence of an offence which at that time was capital.

Mrs Haviland, a native of Ireland, and a lady of great talents, died at Beaconsfield, at an advanced age in October 1807. She was the widow of General Haviland. Her talents were lively, keen and powerful; her acquaintance with elegant literature, extensive and various; she possessed considerable genius; her style was polished, pointed and sparkling; her conversation rich, entertaining and instructive, abounding with anecdote; and her memory retained many beautiful fragments of poetry, some of which seem to have escaped the most assiduous collectors. Above all, her heart was benevolent, friendly and affectionate, and she discharged the duties of a long life in a manner which peculiarly endeared her to those who were more immediately connected with her.

The name of *Rolfe* is frequent in the parish annals particularly from the late eighteenth century and the boundary stone at Holtspur is a memorial to John Rolfe, who at Aylesbury Assizes in 1822, had confirmed a principle already established of tithing corn in the parish of Beaconsfield, by the tenth cock and eleventh shock.

The Ouseleys bought Hall Barn in 1832. After spending much of his life in India and later as ambassador to the King of Persia, Sir Gore came to live at Hall Barn. He made considerable additions to the house and after his death in 1844 was succeeded by his son Sir Frederick Arthur Gore who was educated at Oxford where he later became Professor of Music. He left Hall Barn in 1846 and was ordained in 1849 founding St Michael's College Tenbury, where his valuable collection of manuscripts, books and scores are in the library there. He died in Hereford in 1889.

At Wilton Park where the Royal Army Education Corps Centre now stands was the home of the *Du Pre* family from 1779-1950. Josias Du Pre was Governor of Madras in 1770 and other members of the family leaders in politics and military service. The house, demolished in 1968, contained some work of the Adam brothers.

Miss Katharine Garvin tells us how, in the early twenties, her father, *J. L. Garvin* (1868-1945) happily married again, bought Gregories Farm House 'a typical manor house' which had belonged to the mother of Edmund Waller. Garve was born in Liverpool of Irish Catholic parents so that he rejoiced to follow in his fellow countryman's bailiff's house. Here he delighted in the outhouses which surrounded the house and where most of his books were stored. Here too he wrote the first three volumes of Joseph Chamberlain's life, edited the fourteenth edition of the Encyclopaedia Britannica and continued to edit 'The Observer'.

Enid Blyton lived at Green Hedges in Penn Road for many years where now new houses stand. She was, and is, the delight of generations of children if not of their teachers.

ABOVE: Burke's home at Gregories, (Buckinghamshire Collection);
CENTRE: as he required it to appear, and BELOW:
as it became. (Dr G. Wyatt)

ABOVE: A literary party of the kind Burke held at Gregories. This one was at Reynolds' home, but the Burke set were all there: l. to r. Boswell, Johnson, Reynolds, Burke, Garrick, Paoli, Burney, Warton and Goldsmith, (Mansell Collection). BELOW: The busy butler at Wilton Park made out this account in 1808. (County Record Office)

ABOVE: The Lodge at Butlers Court (Gregories), (Bucks Collection), while BELOW: Beaconsfield House (Wilton Park) looked like this in 1787 when the Dupre's lived there, (Dr G. Wyatt). Their arms are alongside.

GARDEN FRONT

Beaconsfield

88

ENTRANCE FRONT

: Two ways of looking at Disraeli, Earl of Beaconsfield,
e third house at Bulstrode. CENTRE: Two views of Wilton
the 19th century, (all BCM), and BELOW RIGHT:
    J. L. Garvin. (Mansell Collection)

South of Beaconsfield in the 1790's. (British Library)

The Quiet Centuries

As the eighteenth century approached, Beaconsfield was still a small settlement. In 1664 Frenchman Soubiere passed through and called the town no more than a large walled borough, and was fearful of highwaymen—the road was still hazardous, and still the less popular of the two routes from London to Oxford. Yet the alehouse keepers and innholders prospered from passing trade, the incidence of those wealthy, artistic and intellectual gentry who had settled on local estates, and the patronage of their many visitors. Farming flourished modestly in the hinterland. The town remained primarily a centre of local trade and agricultural commerce.

The century brought some change, but for largely external reasons. Indeed, for the next two hundred years, Beaconsfield was not to expand as other towns in the county, nor to suffer from either political trauma or later industrial incursions.

The farmers and landowners dominated local affairs; the road improved, and so did the coaches that plied England's highways. The area had already established a reputation for attracting men of means and minds, and as travel eased and speeded, so Beaconsfield benefited. Gradually, the road through the town became more attractive as the obstructive hills were reduced by lighter carriages, and in the eighteenth century Beaconsfield was among the first to benefit from legislation for turnpike trusts. On the other hand, it was late to attract a railhead, whereas the rest of the county was to see substantial change wrought by the revolution in transport. The Great Central did not arrive here until 1906. So the town's life centred on farming, the road, and the newcomers who sought a convenient home in pleasant surroundings, not too far from London. These factors and their consequences ensured that the town retained much of its character throughout the quiet centuries.

In 1706 vagrants were a problem for the town, and that year John Lee, treasurer, was paid £5 for seeing them on their way.

Traffic slowly increased, but the inhabitants were dilatory in maintaining the highway. In 1709 they were presented at court for failing to repair the road from Amersham to Windsor. The same problem arose again the following year, and in 1711 John Holmes of Beaconsfield was in trouble for refusing to work on the roads. Even so, that year the indictment against the people was discharged after a justices' certificate was produced advising that the road was after all sufficiently repaired.

If the roads were eventually made fit for the increasing traffic, the victuallers and alehouse keepers had difficulty in keeping order in their houses, perhaps due to the transient nature of their trade. In 1710, John Birch, victualler, and John Towsey, alehouse keeper and yeoman, were admonished by the court to 'keep good order'. John Holmes remained recalcitrant, and faced an indictment in 1711 for not working on the roads.

But roads and inns were not the only source of trouble. Domestic strife gave ground for the gossips' tongues to wag on 12 July, 1711 when Elizabeth Turner told the court that she had been sent by her master John Olyffe, rector of Hedgerley, to the Dells. They had little good to say of her employers. Elizabeth Dell added: 'there was a couple of madams of them. There was Madam Clarke of Beaconsfield who was come from the dunghill. There is your mistress what is she amiss out of a nannyhouse at London for anything I know . . . or whether your master and she is married.' The Dell servant Sarah Preston called Mrs Olyffe 'a tinckers trull' and all urged Turner to leave the job.

That year Beaconsfield maltster Henry Fellowes was cleared of earlier allegations by John Wood that he had adulterated his beer—due to 'the many defects and insufficiencyes' of the evidence. In 1715 the parish relieved three children for 2s and spent 15s on a new prayer book. That same decade relief for one poor man cost 2d, and 2d was also paid for the extermination of vermin—one hedgehog.

The roads themselves remained the responsibility of the parish, though in earlier times they had relied solely on individual benefactions. Then government stepped in, and in 1719 and 1751 it became possible for trustees to organise local turnpikes, raise tollgates and draw funds for maintenance from travellers.

In the early 18th century mapmaker John Ogilby wrote 'through the woods at 27 miles (from the Standard at Cornhill) you enter Beaconsfield, situate on a dry hill though no considerable ascent, numbering about a hundred well-built houses, affording several good inns, such as the Swan.'

In 1715 the turnpike between Tyburn and Uxbridge had been approved by Parliament, but in 1717 it was alleged that traffic took the route westwards to avoid the Tyburn tollgate. Two years later the Stokenchurch-Beaconsfield turnpike was enacted, and in 1751 the Uxbridge-Beaconsfield turnpike completed the road link to London through the town. Thereafter the roads attracted revenues, improved greatly, and brought increased trade.

Meanwhile the Oxford stage drew horses in one case from Wattleton Farm and in 1724 Joseph Bates held the lease of the tolls, paying £364 5s.

Law and order were enforced here as elsewhere by recourse to the cage, stocks and whipping post. In 1762 and again in 1778 the local court required that the former be repaired forthwith and a whipping post be erected.

In 1799 Copplestone noted that he was robbed by two mounted highwaymen between Uxbridge and Beaconsfield. That year Beaconsfield even had a dual carriageway beyond the inn at Holtspur. Waggons passed through the town from such places as Woodstock, Banbury, Bicester and Brecon.

Towards the end of the century, a minor event took place at the Saracen's Head on December 27, 1792 which in a way typified the nature of the town. Neighbouring landowners, clergy and the nobility, together with prominent residents, solemnly declared themselves against seditious writings arising from the disturbing effects of the French Revolution, and pledged themselves to root out scurrilous pamphlets and to bring the writers and distributors to book. Beaconsfield was a centre for those who cared for the continuing order of the monarchy and the British way of life.

But change was in the air, and while religious dissent was already no stranger, the thinking men of Beaconsfield acted according to their faith as the 18th century town opened up. The Society of Friends was already established at nearby Jordans, but nonconformity had not gripped Beaconsfield as it had other neighbouring communities. Lollardy had impinged on the town in the 15th and 16th centuries, and rector Andrewes had had his say about 'Puritanisme' in Stuart times.

Dissenting meeting houses recorded by the court of 1707 included one at the home of

Samuel Clarke, schoolmaster, another at that of Daniel Bovingdon and in 1710, one at the home of John Cock. Samuel Clarke had been schoolmaster since 1704 and in 1715 he was also recorded as pastor of a congregation of 180 at the Presbyterian church meeting in Bell Barn since 1704.

In 1725 a Congregational community came together, with Rev Joseph Davies as pastor and meeting in a barn at Butlers Court. Shortly after 1730 a new building replaced the barn, the grounds of which were enlarged in 1741, joined by a vestry in a cottage bought in 1769. The church was known as 'Old Meeting'. Between 1783 and 1830 Beaconsfield acquired its first Sunday School, through John Anthony, a leading Congregationalist. 'Old Meeting' was in use until 1838.

A splinter group formed in 1797, meeting in William Wade's cottage—he was a 'clog and pattern maker'. Rector Dr Stebbings ordered the parish constable to disperse the meetings without success. Their Bethesda Chapel was built by 1800—in fields behind Aylesbury End—and extended in 1808.

In 1833 the original church was reorganised, at 'Old Meeting' and joined the splinter group by 1853, thus reuniting the two congregations.

Settled at the Chapel near Aylesbury End, which had been bought by the Society for the Propagation of the Gospel in the County Districts of England, a branch of the Hackney College Trustees, the congregation acquired more land on the site, and a new church—today's United Reformed Church—was erected for £1500 in 1874/5. The old Chapel became the schoolroom, extended in the 1880s. A manse was built on a new site in Lakes lane in 1896, sold in 1946 and replaced by the first of two in Grove road. A new classroom was added in 1946.

By 1881 there was also a Wesleyan Chapel in a converted ribbon factory, and a temporary Primitive Methodist chapel off Windsor End near the old school. The earliest known Wesleyan Reform Chapel was in Factory Yard in 1852. The Reformers fought off a determined bid by a newcomer, just after they had repaired and decorated their chapel in 1865, and acquired the present site in 1898, started building in 1899 and opened the present Methodist Chapel in 1900.

The old Parish Church was showing signs of wear and depredations by the time the Bishop visited in the early 18th century and in 1720 repairs cost over £50. The building was restored, indeed largely rebuilt in 1869.

While Beaconsfield developed churches to care for the town's spiritual needs, local men and women were concerned for the physical welfare of the less fortunate. Beaconsfield had long since become a caring community, with charities established by such as Thomas Bawell, Nicholas Cooke, Richard Nedham, George Hanford, Henry Clowberry, Lady Anne Hyde and Philip, 4th Baron Wharton—not forgetting Waller's son Edmund.

In 1728 Frances Waller left £500 for property investment to fund clothing for the poor, and in 1779 surgeon Thomas Read left incomes for bread for those poor 'on Christmas Day for ever', while in 1810 another Edmund Waller provided the means to bread, clothing and blankets for the needy of the parish.

Other charitable bequests were those of Mary Stevenson in 1812 and of her sister Elizabeth Sarah in 1830, respectively for those not receiving alms, and the especially hard cases.

John Stransum put his family vault's upkeep first in his bequests of 1837, but then directed that six poor widows should benefit from the residue, and in 1886 Charles Harford left precise instructions to fund any dispensary, infirmary, hospital or convalescent home, to fund nurses, patients' travel expenses, and to supply clothing, bedding, fuel and other medical aid. In 1891 Mary Thompson of Sandhurst made similar provisions. (Only seven years ago the charitable tradition of the town was maintained by the formation of the Margaret Puckle Memorial Trust.)

At the opening of the nineteenth century, the town held 1,149 people, traffic still thundered through on the London-Oxford road, and the inns continued to prosper. The market was now in decline, but the fairs on Candlemas Day and Holy Thursday continued, Burke had died and his widow lived on at Gregories; the Wallers of Hall Barn would soon be replaced (in 1832) by the Gore-Ouseleys, and the Dupre's had owned Wilton Park since 1770.

In 1802 the parish erupted with anger when William Wellings had the presumption to build against the wall of the workhouse, shutting out the daylight. Taxed with his thoughtless act, he promised to put it right—by altering the workhouse.

Fourteen years later the worthies of the parish decided to rebuild the cage in the courtyard of that same workhouse, but first they sought the approval of Miss Charsley, who owned the site. Back came the unequivocal answer that she 'absolutely objects'. As it had already been agreed that the cage on its previous site 'appears to every inhabitant of this town to have led to great and offensive nuisance', approaches must be made to the lord of the manor to agree to a site north of the market house. For good measure, the stocks were to go there too. So far as we know, this time the scheme was approved.

In 1822, some twenty years before the ancient tithe system was finally commuted for cash considerations, Beaconsfield's rector Rev John Gould took John Rolfe to Aylesbury Assizes —and lost. He had unsuccessfully disputed the ancient Beaconsfield custom of tithing 'by the tenth cock and eleventh shock'. The rector's living was then worth £750 a year. By 1847 it had been sequestered, and a curate (John Bradford) appointed—at £150 a year.

In 1826 the vestry reported that the roads were in 'an excellent state of repair' but four years later a commentator wrote that Beaconsfield was 'once important for the grain and meal trade', that the lace trade was 'depressed' and only some papermaking remained. Most of that was well outside the town at Wooburn and at Loudwater.

In 1830 the taverns included the Cross Keys (landlord Richard Herbert), Elm Tree (Joseph Lipscomb), Greyhound (David Blake), Hare (George Fox), Swan (Joshua Grimmett), Weavers' Arms (Jno. Jezuph) and the White Horse (Mary Hutcheson).

James Hurst and John Jackson made watches in Wycombe End and London street, there were four wheelwrights, a straw hatmaker (Mary Chapman), miller (James Rance) and a brickmaker (Jno. Stransham).

The road was busy. Coaches called daily. The Royal Mail from Worcester thundered into the George; the Oxonian from Shrewsbury called at the Saracen's Head; the Star came through from Woodstock. Tolletts Coaches from nearby Wycombe called twice daily at the White Hart except on Sundays. Joshua Grimmett provided a waggon service from his High street premises, while another seven out-of-town carriers plied through the town.

There were several private schools. Cecilia Boddy and her husband provided separate education for day and boarding girls and boys, while Rev William Mussage boarded boys only. Jeremiah and Mary Hartnell, and Joseph Jezuph each ran a further small establishment.

In 1837 the tolls yielded £3,580, though in the next 10 years this decreased to £1,600. By 1846 almshouses existed between Lacks (Lakes) lane and London road, and between 1871 and 1891 the inhabitants were moved into cottages. In 1870 the remaining fair was redated to 10 May, since when it has always been held on that date. In 1873 an educational explosion hit the town, when the Boys', Girls' and Infants' National Schools were built, accommodating altogether 268 children, though they were designed for 350. There remained two private schools: Miss Selina Bolton's ladies' school at Leigh House, and Arthur Denman's school for 'sons of gentlemen' at the School House. By 1881 the population had risen to 1,635 but that included part of Coleshill. The police station at Windsor End was manned by Inspector John Chaplin and two constables, and by 1889 was one of only thirteen in the whole county.

Farming still played a major part in the local economy in 1888, and if the industrial revolution had not entirely bypassed the town, it had certainly made more impact at neighbouring Wycombe and at Aylesbury and Chesham. George Smyth Gower ran a farming and engineering implement business in the High street, James Honour manufactured hurdles and birch brooms at Widgenton Farm, William Lynn maintained the centuries' old local tradition of brick, lime and tile making at Nipland's Kiln, and William Harding managed to make a few chairs at his grocer's premises in the High Street.

There were then ten farmers; thirteen inns, alehouses and vintners; five builders, plumbers and carpenters; two blacksmiths; thirty two shopkeepers; corn and coal merchants, a watchmaker (Walter Frederick Porter), boot and shoe makers, saddlers, wheelwrights and a cooper.

There was one lodging house run by Joseph Shelton in the High Street and the legal tradition of the town was maintained by George Alfred and George Henry Charsley, while Richard Hedges practised as a surveyor and William Henry Brecknell was the town's surgeon. One carrier remained—A. Roberts & Co.

Meanwhile the railway revolution was nearing the town. By 1876 Wooburn Green station, two and a half miles distant, was the nearest point on the Great Western line to town. In 1850 the local Board of Health had taken responsibility for local administration, and in 1894 the Urban District Council replaced it. In its last year, the Board raised a rate of 3d in the pound for highway maintenance, and successfully borrowed a steamroller from the County, free of charge.

By 1901 the population was down—to 1,570, but that excluded Coleshill.

In 1906 the railway came, and Beaconsfield found itself on the joint Great Western and Great Central line, with suburban trains to Paddington and Marylebone.

Beaconsfield, which had staved off development and industry, and prospered quietly for two centuries from the coach trade, now faced the railway age.

An exact List of all the Stage Coaches and Carriers, with the Names of the Towns they come from, and their respective Inns in London, and the Days they go out: Very useful for Shopkeepers and Tradesmen.

A

AYLSBURY Carrier, Sarazen's Head on *Snow-hill*, and Crown in *Warwick-lane*, Wednesday. Coach, Crown in *Holborn*, Monday, Wednesday, and Friday; Black Swan *Holborn*, Tuesday, Thursday, and Saturday.

Amersham Carrier, Angel *St. Giles's Church*, sat.
Acton Coach, Talbot in the *Strand*, every Day.
St. Alban's Carrier, Bell *Aldersgate-street*, mond. wednes. fri. Coach *ditto*, tues. thurs. sat.

Abingdon Carrier, White Horse *Friday-street*, fri. Sarazen's Head *Friday-street*, thurs. Coach at the same Places tues. thurs. sat.

Ashford Carrier, Star *Fish-street-hill*, thurs.
Ampton Carrier, Cock *Aldersgate-street*, thurs.
Amptil Carrier, White Hart *Aldersg. str.* wednes. Pewter Platter *St. John's-street*, thurs.

Arundell Carrier, Queen's Head *Southwark*, mon. wednes.

Ashbourn Carrier, Castle *Woodstreet*, mon.
Andover Carrier, King's Arms *Holborn-bridge*, thurs. Coach White Horse *Fleet-street*, mon. thurs.
Ashdon Carrier, 2 Swans without *Bishopsg.* tues.
St. Asaph Carrier, Castle and Faulcon *Aldersgate-street*, mon. thurs.

Abostongly Carrier, George *Holborn* Conduit, wednes. fri.

Aldenham Carrier, White Horse *Holborn bridge*, wednes.

Ashwel Carrier, Katherine Wheel *Bishopsgate*, tues. Cock *Old-street*, tues.

Ashby de la Zouch Carrier, Ax *Aldermanbury*, mon.

Answick Carrier, White Horse by *Cripplegate*, mon.

Adderstone Carrier, Castle *Smithfield Bars*, mon.

B

Bath and *Bristol* Coach, Bell in *Bell Savage Yard Ludgate-hill*, wednes. thurs. Bell *Strand*, mon. thurs. Chequer *Charing-cross*, and Cross Keys *Gracechurch-street*, mon. thurs. Coach and Horses in the *Strand*, and 3 Cups *Bread-street* ditto. Flying Coach, Chequer *Charing-cross*, mon. wedn. fri.

Burford Carrier, Bell *Friday-street*, thurs.
Basingstoke Carrier, Bell Savage *Ludgate-hill* and White Horse by the Ditch Side, fri.
Blichmaly Carrier, Half Moon *Southwark*, sat.
Buckingham Carrier, Sarazen's Head *Carter-lane*, wednes. George *Smithfield*, Bell *Warwick lane*, ditto. Cock *Old-street*, tues.

Brentford Coach, Bolt and Tun *Fleet-street*, and Red Lion *Fetter-lane*, every Day.

Barnet Coach, Cross Keys *St. John's-street*, twice a Day.

Bridgenorth Coach, Blue Boar *High Holborn*, mon.

Baldock Carrier, Red Lion *Red-cross-street*, tues. fri.

Biscister Carrier, Black Bull *Holborn*, wednes. fri. Oxford Arms *Warwick-lane*, wednes. Coach, Bell *Strand*, mon. thurs.

Brackley Carrier, White Swan *Holborn-bridge*, thurs.

Blanford Carrier, Rose *Holborn-bridge*, mon. wednes. Bell *Friday-street*, mon.

Bradford Carrier, White Horse *Cripplegate*, thurs.
Beaconsfield Carrier, Bell *Warwick lane*, tues.
Bedford Carrier, Windmill, Pewter Platter, and Swan with 2 Necks, *St. John's-street*, wednes. Red Lion *Aldersgate-street*, Rose *Smithfield*, thurs. Coach, Windmill *St. John's-street*, thurs. Red Lion *Aldersgate-street*, tues. fri.

Brentwood Carrier, 2 Nuns, sat. and Blue Boar without *Aldgate*, wednes. ... Blue Boar ... and Cross ...

ABOVE: Before the road came into focus again, there was only one carrier, and no stage coach recorded—in 1720, and BELOW: later, when the Royal Mail came from London, this is how it looked.
(Both Mansell Collection)

ABOVE: The Beaconsfield and Stokenchurch Turnpike Trust files its accounts in 1835, (County Record Office), and BELOW: the Tally-Ho stage coach was still about in Beaconsfield in 1926! (D. R. Fletcher)

April y^e 17: 1728 *[handwritten receipt]* Then received of M^r
Fellows & Mr Bunion five Pounds being in full
for remaking Beconfields Church Clock
J Say received by me John Thompson

There have been many mills; this one survived until recently (Bucks
Collection), while clockmaker John Jackson Jnr. worked in Wycombe End
in 1830 (Lord Burnham) and John Thompson repaired the church clock
in 1728. (County Record Office)

98

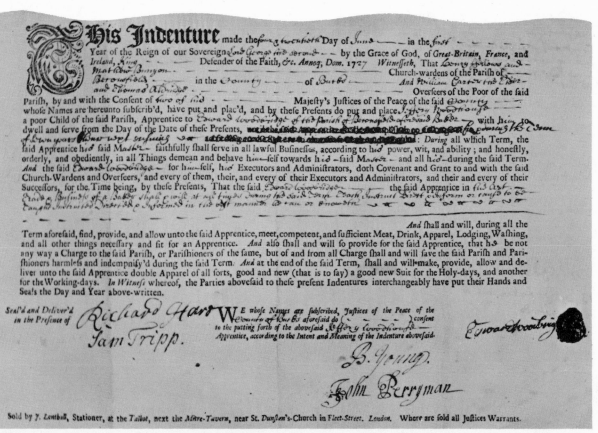

ABOVE: Business flourished in 1727 when Jeffrey Woodhouse was apprenticed to Beaconsfield's Edward Woodbridge, (County Record Office), and BELOW: H. Perfect mended your boots in Wycombe End at the turn of this century. (John Harding)

99

LEFT: The 1740 list of residents, tenants and suitors within the Manor of
Beaconsfield, (County Record Office), and RIGHT: the
Burnham Hundred in 1756. (BCM)

Account of the Expences of Elizabeth
Chandler Lying in at Beaconsfield Bucks
1765
Nov. 17: To a pint of Brandy — X — 0. 2. 0
            To a horse & Man to Uxbridge
            for the Docter _____ 0. 2. 6
    18: To a horse & Man to Uxbridge 0. 2. 6
         To a pint of Brandy — X — 0. 2. 0
         To the Docter Bill _____ 1. 8. 0
         To the Mann midwife Bill X 3. 8. 0
         To the Nurses Bill _____ 0. 12. 0
         To th Hean Bill _____ 0. 5. 0
                                     £5. 14. 0
    Mr Richmond charges going to Uxbridge
    twice _____ .. 5 .. 0
                                     £5. 19. 0
         Paid John Fellows
              & Anthony _____

Mr Dames Bill 1761
July the 14 Pare of Stays for Suzan Grace 0 = 4 0
Apl the 14 1762 Reced of Full Contents
         of This Bill By ad Mark of
Ann Field X

LEFT: Evidence of local craft, this cherry basket and ladder hook
were used on Seelys Farm, (BCM), while RIGHT: Elizabeth Chandler's
lying-in cost £5 19s in 1765, and BELOW: Ann Field charged Suzan Grace
4s for stays in 1761. (Both County Record Office)

101

ABOVE: Jeffreys' map of the district in 1770, (BCM), and BELOW: an
18th century account for church repairs. (County Record Office)

ABOVE: An early print of the church, (Rev Dr Wright), and BELOW: a
hill rose up unexpectedly in this 1818 drawing. (BCM)

ABOVE LEFT: The Parish Church in 1847, RIGHT: After the 19th century
restoration (Rev Dr Wright), and BELOW RIGHT: today.

BELOW LEFT: Factory Yard, and CENTRE: the later Congregational
Church in Aylesbury End (Rev Dr Wright).

The Names of the Members of the Congregational Church of Christ at Beaconsfield Bucks who meet together in the Name of Christ to worship God in Spirit & in Truth & to walk together in the fear of the Lord & in the Faith & order of the Gospel. November 5 1768

Abrm Darby — Minister Dead   Mrs Darby — Deced
David Anthony Dead   Mrs Mary Anthony Dead
George Floyd Dead   Mrs Floyd Dead
Thomas Knight Dead   Mrs Knight Dead
John Anthony Dead   Mrs Anthony Jno Dead
Thomas Insworth Dead   Mrs Insworth Deced
Henry Nash Dead   Mrs Nash Dead
Willm Seabrook Dismissed   Mrs Seabrook absented
Willm Anthony Deced
Willm Hatch absent   Mrs Hatch Dead
Daniel Anthony   Mrs Anthony Suspended
———— Wright   Mrs Wright
Paul King Dead   Mrs King Dead
John Smith Dead   Mrs Smith Dead
James Lovett Dead   Mrs Lovett Dead
    Mrs Elizabeth Day Deced
James Hall Deced   Mrs Hall Dead
Thomas Lovett absented   Mrs Hannah Lovett absented

ABOVE: The Congregational community in 1768, (County Record Office)
and BELOW: the interior of the church at the turn of the century,
(Rev Dr Wright)

ABOVE : The chapel in Shepherds Lane, and BELOW : material comforts at the Red Lion, Knotty Green. (John Harding)

107

ABOVE: Rev Bradford's house, as sketched by Buckler in 1832, (British Library), and BELOW: The Old Post House of the age of elegance.

ABOVE: Wendover House and BELOW: Wycombe End House, both
dominant features of Beaconsfield's 18th century legacy.

LEFT: Frederick Charsley in 1844, and RIGHT: Rocque's 18th century
map of the district, (both BCM), and BELOW: the lock-up
at Aylesbury End. (D. R. Fletcher)

LEFT: Eighteenth century Beaconsfield tavern account, (County Record Office), and RIGHT: the old Cross Keys, Wycombe End, now an antique shop, (D. R. Fletcher), with BELOW: another of the town's ports of call, the Greyhound, Windsor End.

111

The later Star PH and beyond it, the Old Hare, in Aylesbury End.

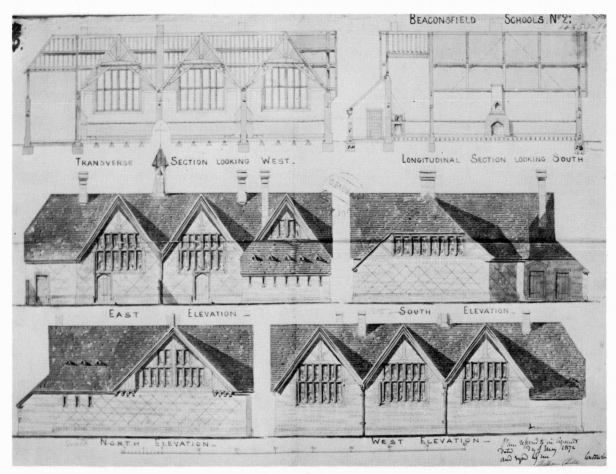

ABOVE: The 1872 design for the school (County Record Office), and
BELOW: sadder days 102 years later.

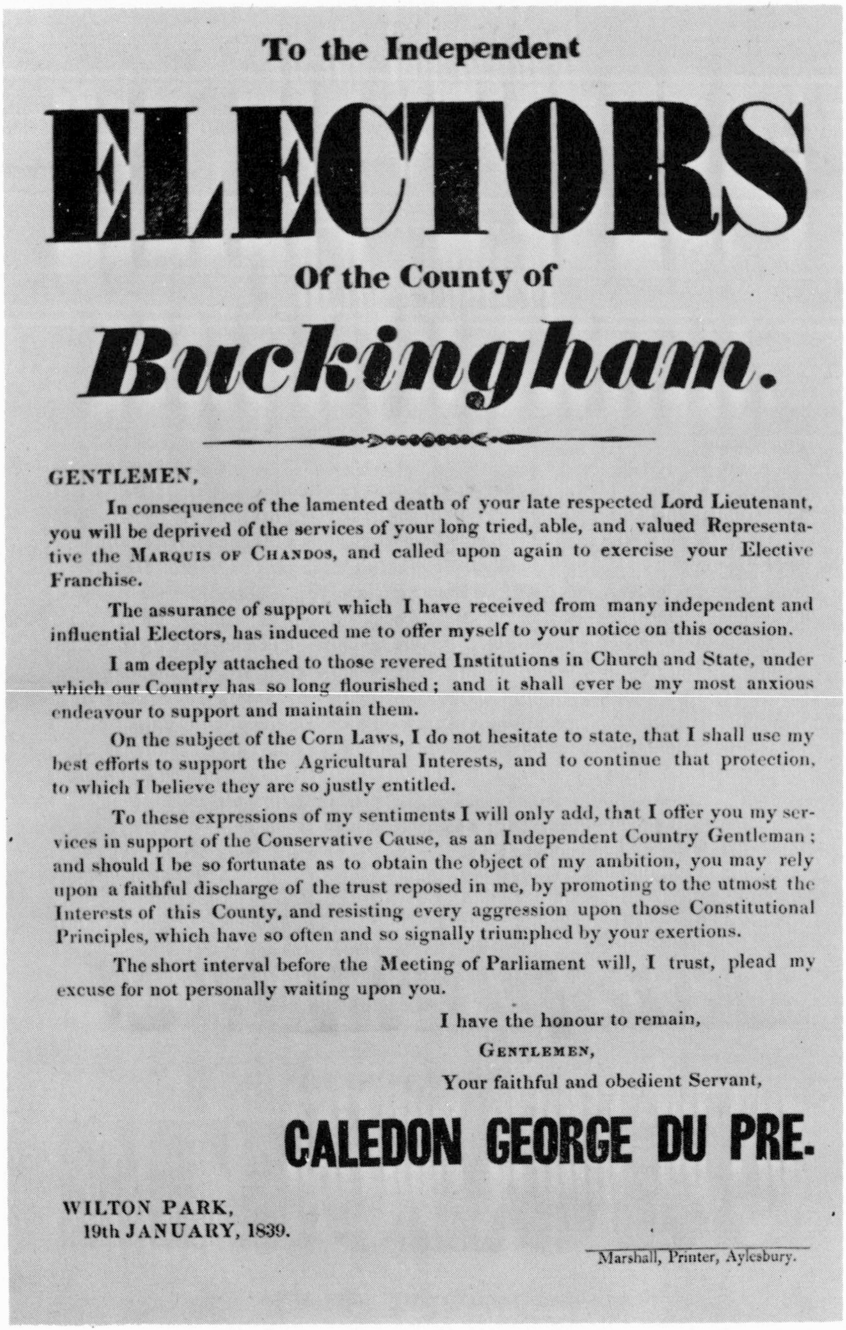

To the Independent

ELECTORS

Of the County of

Buckingham.

GENTLEMEN,

In consequence of the lamented death of your late respected Lord Lieutenant, you will be deprived of the services of your long tried, able, and valued Representative the MARQUIS OF CHANDOS, and called upon again to exercise your Elective Franchise.

The assurance of support which I have received from many independent and influential Electors, has induced me to offer myself to your notice on this occasion.

I am deeply attached to those revered Institutions in Church and State, under which our Country has so long flourished; and it shall ever be my most anxious endeavour to support and maintain them.

On the subject of the Corn Laws, I do not hesitate to state, that I shall use my best efforts to support the Agricultural Interests, and to continue that protection, to which I believe they are so justly entitled.

To these expressions of my sentiments I will only add, that I offer you my services in support of the Conservative Cause, as an Independent Country Gentleman; and should I be so fortunate as to obtain the object of my ambition, you may rely upon a faithful discharge of the trust reposed in me, by promoting to the utmost the Interests of this County, and resisting every aggression upon those Constitutional Principles, which have so often and so signally triumphed by your exertions.

The short interval before the Meeting of Parliament will, I trust, plead my excuse for not personally waiting upon you.

I have the honour to remain,

GENTLEMEN,

Your faithful and obedient Servant,

CALEDON GEORGE DU PRE.

WILTON PARK,
19th JANUARY, 1839.

Marshall, Printer, Aylesbury.

Caledon George Du Pre appeals to county electors
from Beaconsfield, 1839. (BCM)

ABOVE: The police station and court house of 1870 and BELOW: shades of
elegance in London End. (D. R. Fletcher)

The Surveyor's Report was not ready for this earlier Meeting but he produced a letter from the County Council Surveyor of the 7th December 1894 that the Council's Steam Roller would in due course be allowed to the Board free of cost and that if the work proposed necessitated material in excess of the triennial outlay the excess would be recommended to be allowed

The last minute of the Board of Health in 1894—the county's steamroller is available at no charge.

116

ABOVE: The Plough and cottages in Windsor End, since demolished, and
BELOW: London End. (Both John Harding)

117

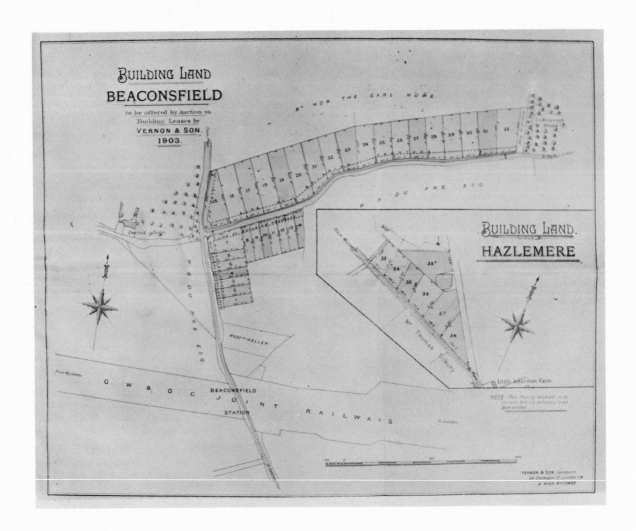

ABOVE: In 1903, the railway was planned, and sites were on offer in
Ledborough lane, (BCM), while BELOW: Windsor End wore a deserted air
seen from the site of today's roundabout. (Bucks Collection)

From This Day Forth

If Beaconsfield's shape was determined in the 17th century, and reinforced in the succeeding two hundred years, the coming of the railway extended rather than changed the town. Traditionally an attractive and accessible place of residence rather than of commerce, it now became doubly so. The new railway link brought not only London, but the Midlands and North within easy reach, and the London-Oxford Road's dominance was soon over-taken by its cheap and rapid competitor. Shops sprang up near the station and houses multiplied, to give meaning to the New Town, away from the original settlement.

In the first two decades of the twentieth century, the town's population doubled. One unforeseen influx of newcomers was the major intake of Belgian refugees from the Great War, and this had more than one impact on the growing town. Until then, Catholics were not numerous in Beaconsfield, and the faith which left the area with the Dissolution had only emerged again in a small way back in 1878—when Sir Philip Rose Bt built a private chapel at Rayners, Penn. Now Sir Philip's chapel was hopelessly inadequate for the tem-porarily enlarged congregation.

For two Sundays Mass was said in Burnham Hall, and then worship moved to the assembly room behind the Railway Hotel, afterwards to become part of the renamed Earl of Beacons-field PH. Apart from a short period when worshippers attended Mass at Lord Burnham's Lodge, this became the 'church' for several years, even after the refugees returned to their homes in 1919. Meanwhile a site for a permanent church had been acquired in Woodside Avenue, but eventually after financial hardship, and other locations were considered, the present site in Warwick Road was bought and the church opened in 1927, though it was five more years before a resident priest was appointed—Monsignor G. W. Smith. In 1934 a hall project was born, subsequently replaced by a larger building—Borlase Hall. St Joseph's Nursing Home at Fernhurst owed its origins to the community in that same year. In 1938 Chesterton died, and subsequently the Chestertons bequeathed their home Top Meadow in Grove Road to the Catholic community. It is now a temporary home for convert Anglican clergymen and nuns, administered by the Catholic Converts' Aid Society. The church itself was extended in memory of Chesterton in 1939 and the complete building consecrated in 1947.

Meanwhile Burnham Abbey, formed in 1266 and dissolved in 1539, passed through various hands, until in 1914 it was restored for convent use and the altar reconsecrated in 1915. In 1916 The Society of the Precious Blood took possession and thereafter the Priory maintained its activities as a religious house.

The Baptist cause appears to have first been raised in 1908, and services started in a bor-rowed hall—an old garage—two years later. But financial difficulties delayed matters. Next year the garage was sold and the congregation met in New Town Hall, their first minister being appointed a year later. In 1913 the church was formed, in 1914 the Sunday school started and in 1915 the Baptist Chapel was opened, at an initial cost of nearly £2000.

In the Anglican parish, the daughter church of St Thomas, Holtspur was opened in what is now the church hall, in 1949, and the present building in Mayflower Way consecrated in 1961. Years earlier in 1937 the Congregational community opened a Sunday School in the sports pavilion opposite the King's Head, moving to private rooms in 1939. A temporary wooden building was erected in North Drive in 1946 and the church at Crabtree Close opened in 1961.

In 1910 Beaconsfield saw a further expression of the town's traditional care for the needy, when Miss Edith Hennell and Miss Gladys Meates founded, with the help of others including Bertha and Katherine Meates, a Children's Convalescent Home for the recovery of sick children at Great Ormond Street Hospital, in a house provided by Miss Hennell, itself built on the site of the old Workhouse in the High Street (now Peter Knight's shop). There were beds for some twenty patients. Many of the children arrived in near-starvation condition, recovering at a cost to the home of 1s 5d a child.

Extensions were in hand in 1912, adding six beds, and a year later the neighbouring house was acquired, adding five more cots, and more London hospitals sent their sick children to the Home.

In the Great War 89 Belgian refugees were housed at one time or another, until local homes were provided for them. The Home had room for 36 'inmates' and launched an appeal for funds to maintain the children and refugees in their care—one of many such efforts down the years, often labelled 'Save the Babies!' Parents where the father was serving abroad, were charged the fare of 1s 6d to send their children, and the age limits were five for boys and 10 for girls. There were seven staff and the annual costs ran to £1000. Sixty or 70 children were boarded out, but in the care of the Home's staff.

When a munitions factory exploded in Silvertown on 19 January, 1917, the Home once again offered refuge to 34 homeless children of the tragedy. That same year an appeal was launched for £10,000 to extend. Chesterton himself stepped in with help financially, and through publicising the Home's needs. In 1922 the Home moved to White Barn accomodating 22 children and in 1925 the building (now the site of Hughes' Garage), was substantially extended. The Shaftesbury Society donated £1000 of the White Barn purchase cost and became trustees. The age limit was set at five for both sexes. On 23 April, 1931 Queen Mary paid the Home a visit. Throughout its history the Burnhams were active in their support and patronage.

In 1932 the Home reported an annual 217 children cared for, 24 of them at no charge at all. Costs had risen to £2208 per annum, of which only £573 was spent on staff and £36 on administration. In 1935 the Home reported that the children cared for had risen to 240, a total of 4000 since its foundation. Costs were still only £2350 per annum, staff actually costing less, and administration only one pound more. In January 1941 Miss Gladys Meates died, and in December 1946 Edith Hennell died. Miss Hennell handed the home over to the Shaftesbury Society on 2 May, 1942.

Charity finds many forms and in 1923 a Beaconsfield model railway enthusiast, Roland Callingham, acquired a field next door to his property in Warwick Road, and found local people using it as a rubbish tip. He used the rubble dumped there as the basis of a rockery, and then started building. But unlike the other enthusiasts who built in that same road— where St Michael's Church was to rise to serve the New Town in 1914, reaching completion in 1955, this entrepeneur's buildings were child-sized. He built what has become world famous as Bekonscot Model Village—a corruption of Beaconsfield and Ascot, where Callingham once lived, opening it in 1929. He died in 1961.

The model village has done much good, and caused some local irritation. With its 2500 ft of rail track, 40,000 sq ft of 'development', 75 buildings and 8000 fir trees, 25 per cent of which are replanted each year to keep their miniature scale, it has so far attracted over six million visitors and raised over £228,000 for charity locally and elsewhere. It is run by Trustees as a Charitable Association, and lives on a knife edge. For residents, annoyed by parking, noise and litter, in 1954 secured a High Court injunction through the County Council for the village's complete clearance—back to the 1923 state of the site. Extensions of temporary planning permission have been granted since then so that the village stays put at least until 1979. Now many influential residents hope it will stay for good—objectors at recent hearings have reduced, and few have been strictly local.

As Beaconsfield expanded, and its institutions increased in number, scope and variety, the emphasis was on the New Town and outlying districts. The original settlement resisted change, doubtless to the delight of the many weekend visitors of our day, and there developed two towns within one urban district. Not a unique phenomenon in South Bucks, Beaconsfield is effectively two places linked by a road—the old town centred on the original four 'Ends' and the New Town clustered round the railway station.

War took its toll of the community, and the memorial, originally on the axis of the Ends and now moved down Windsor End, remembers the fallen of both wars. A reminder of the defence needs of our own times lies within the old Wilton Park estate. The Royal Army Educational Corps occupies the buildings that have replaced the old mansion on a different site within the estate.

The RAEC Centre moved to the town in 1950 as the Army School of Education, designated the Centre in 1970. It comprises a Headquarters and three functional schools: The Army School of Education, the Army School of Languages and the Army School of Instructional Technology. The Headquarters coordinates and directs the schools and runs the Corps Museum, university liaison, and the Centre Library.

Of the three schools, the first handles the training of RAEC officers and education in support of training for serving soldiers. This includes educational training for Sandhurst entrants, technical education for trades, and RAEC officer education.

The second school covers a variety of languages, including English as a foreign language, such as for members of the Brigade of Gurkhas, Russian, and Arabic. Interpreter Courses cater also for members of the British and Foreign Diplomatic Services.

The third school has three roles: to develop principles and techniques of the technology; to provide consultancy and advisory services on training problems, and improve training techniques; and to provide training and instructional courses. With its post-graduate expertise, audio-visual research and design, closed circuit TV developments, retrieval systems, and programmed learning techniques, it is an example of the sophistication of today's Army, and of the traditional role of Beaconsfield in attracting men of intellect.

Six years after the Army moved into Wilton Park, international industry took over another of Beaconsfield's old mansions, Butlers Court. Wiggins Teape, UK based world paper manufacturers and converters, established their Research and Development Centre there, for Beaconsfield offered rapid access, convertible buildings and ideal pilot plant space.

Butlers Court today houses some 225 staff, who pursue the development of improved production processes and new products and process enquiries, analyse markets, research the structure of paper itself. Butlers Court originated the process for producing polymer coated photographic paper, which won the Company the Queen's Award in 1975. In 1959, South Bucks Typesetters Ltd, was established in Aylesbury End—a new local industry to serve media and literature; in 1976 they helped to produce this book.

One development which in 1976 caused some soul-searching has not come to pass. In 1974 the old urban district was merged with other authorities including Gerrards Cross, Burnham, Iver, Denham and the Eton rural district, and today the authority goes under the name of the South Bucks District Council. The council works from Slough offices, but in the seventies plans were formulated for a major complex in the New Town. Then it seemed that by the 1980s Beaconsfield would have one of the most modern administrative centres in Bucks, but it was not to be. Today the combined district is home to some 62,000 people. The estate developments at Wattleton Road, Seeleys, Sandelswood End and near Forty Green have grown apace in the last decade, and a major development is scheduled for completion this autumn, when the John Lewis Partnership opens its new supermarket on the old Earl of Beaconsfield site — a site for which the company paid £1.35m — and brings new employment for 130 people.

Now Beaconsfield faces the uncertainties of the future with clear advantages. The original settlement wears a settled and relatively calm face, unspoilt by speculators or planners; the New Town taps roots that go back seventy years; Hall Barn sits immaculately on the town's outskirts, a constant reminder of the poetry of the past; Chesterton's work and faith lives on between old and new town, in a sense linking both, and the New Town itself bustles with modern shops, a fast commuter rail link, and its civic centre on the horizon.

Beaconsfield, as for so many centuries, sits astride the route to metropolis, home to men and women of minds and means, and a contrast between the departed age of elegance and the modern age of affluence.

The town gathers in Wycombe End for George V's Coronation in 1911
(D. R. Fletcher)

ABOVE: The railway opened up the town in 1906—before that these men cut, dug and carried, with pick, shovel and barrow; they came from many parts, such as Ireland, Norfolk and Cumberland, and many settled —their descendants still live here. (R. J. Cyster Jolly Cricketers, Seer Green). BELOW: Station road was well defined by the '20s. (D. R. Fletcher)

ABOVE: Penn road acquired a bank and the Railway Hotel, (John Harding) and BELOW: the Earl of Beaconsfield is no more.

ABOVE: Commercial development near the station, and BELOW: the
Catholic church in Warwick road.

LEFT: Beaconsfield's Baptist Church. RIGHT ABOVE: Edith M. Hennel
and BELOW: Gladys Meates. (Dorothy Collins)

126

ABOVE: On the old workhouse site this building in 1910 became the
Convalescent Home, and BELOW: The Shelter at the
Home. (Dorothy Collins)

127

ABOVE: Nurses Lily Street and Susie Platts with the first six children at
the home, and BELOW: some of Beaconsfield's Belgian
refugees. (Dorothy Collins)

ABOVE: New home from Home—White Barn in 1922, and BELOW: with
the extensions in 1925. (Dorothy Collins)

ABOVE: Bekonscot and its founder, Roland Callingham. (Jarrold & Sons)

BELOW LEFT: St Michael's Church before it was enlarged, and RIGHT: the unveiling of the war memorial in the centre of the crossroads now occupied by the roundabout. (Both D. R. Fletcher)

ABOVE: The memorial in its original position, (Rev Dr Wright), LEFT: on its present site, and BELOW: Wycombe End before these buildings gave way to Festival Green. (D. R. Fletcher)

131

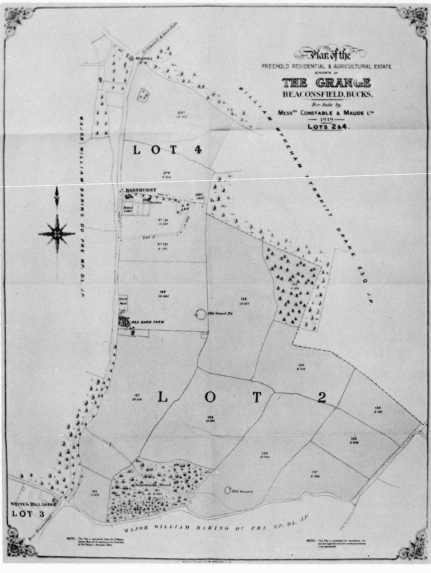

ABOVE: Pre-war Old Town, (Rev Dr Wright) and BELOW: 1919 land
sale. (County Record Office)

132

ABOVE: The "new" Post Office, 1927, (Rev Dr Wright), and BELOW:
the post office when in Windsor End. (D. R. Fletcher)

133

ABOVE: Wycombe End, before the post office moved, and BELOW:
Windsor End, much as we see it today. (Both D. R. Fletcher)

134

ABOVE: Grove road, in somewhat parlous earlier state (Rev Dr Wright)

CENTRE: The Pond at Candlemas Lane before the fence went up, and
BELOW: Malthouse Square, with its sail-less windmill, built in 1811, and
community use of the greensward. (Both D. R. Fletcher)

135

ABOVE: RAEC Centre, Wilton Park (RAEC); LEFT: Butlers Court and
RIGHT: Wiggins Teape research in progress there. (Wiggins Teape)

ABOVE: Beaconsfield's Library and BELOW: the old Council Offices.

South Elevation.

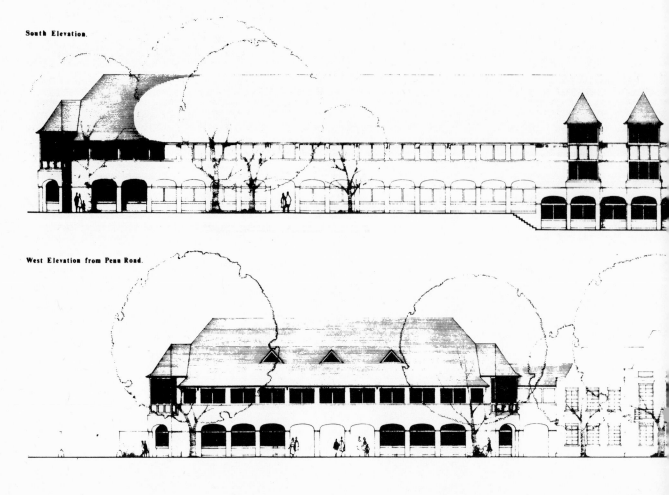

West Elevation from Penn Road.

East Elevation.

Section Through Public Concourse.

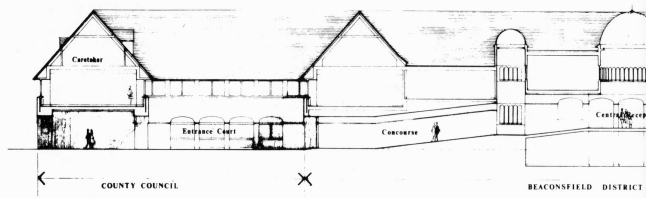

Caretaker

Entrance Court

Concourse

Central Recep

COUNTY COUNCIL

BEACONSFIELD DISTRICT

138

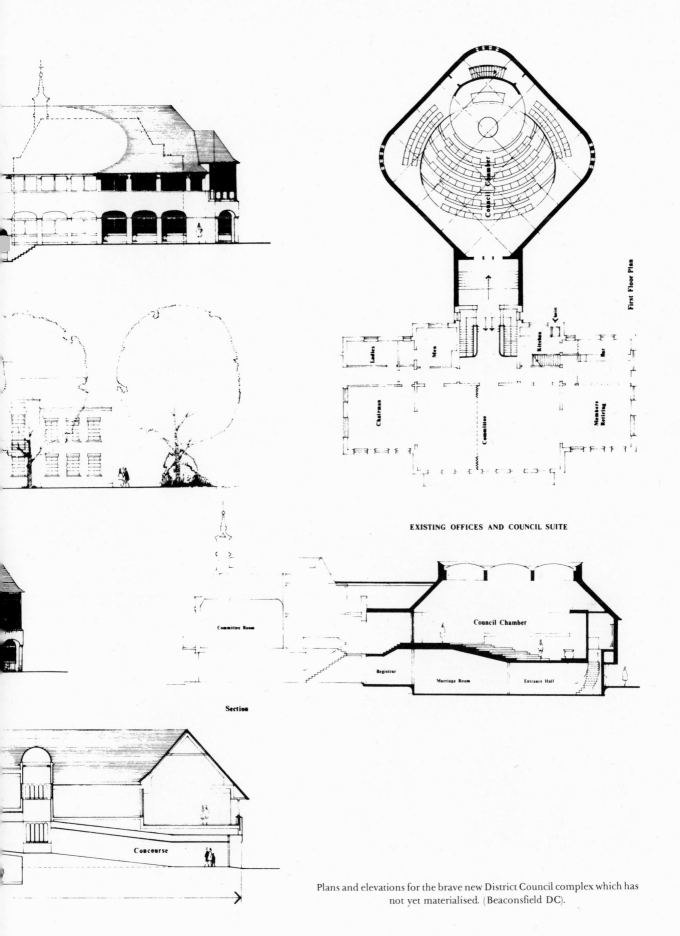

First Floor Plan

Council Chamber

Ladies · Men · Kitchen · Bar

Chairman · Committee · Members Retiring

EXISTING OFFICES AND COUNCIL SUITE

Committee Room

Section

Council Chamber

Registrar · Marriage Room · Entrance Hall

Concourse

Plans and elevations for the brave new District Council complex which has not yet materialised. (Beaconsfield DC).

139

ABOVE: Behind Yew Tree Close today and BELOW: to the rear of 32 London End—two victims of the passing years; the London End warehouse is under threat of demolition.

Still Beaconsfield celebrates its ancient fair, seen here in 1975.

The two faces of Beaconsfield: ABOVE: new town facade, and BELOW: the elegant survivors of the old town.

ENDPAPERS: The grounds at Hall Barn.

Bibliography

Before Beaconsfield
Memoirs of Geological Survey of Gt. Britain, Sheet 225 of the New Series. 1922
Geology of the Country around Beaconsfield. R. L. Sherlock and A. H. Noble.
Ice Ages, Their Nature and Effects. Ian Cornwall. 1970
Pleistocene Geology and Biology. R. G. West. 1968
The Environment of Early Man in the British Isles. J. G. Evans. 1975
Early Man in South Buckinghamshire. J. F. Head. 1955
British Pre-History ed Colin Renfrew. 1974
Iron Age Communities in Britain. Barry Cunliffe. 1974
Britannia. S. S. Frere. 1967
Latimer. Keith Branigan. 1971
Verulamium and the Roman Chilterns. Keith Branigan. 1973
Victoria County History.
Records of Buckinghamshire.
A History of the Parish of Penn. J. G. Jenkins. 1955
Roman Roads in the South East Midlands, by The Viatores. (1964)
The Environment in British Prehistory, ed. Simmons and Tooley. (1981)
Prehistoric Flintwork in Britain, Stephen Pierpoint. (1981)

The Mediaeval Scene
Charters: The Cartulary of Missenden Abbey, ed. J. G. Jenkins (Bucks Record Society,
        Vol. 2)
        Bodleian Library: MS Charters Bucks 886-1199
        Public Record Office
        British Museum
        Westminster Abbey
Manorial Records: BM Harleian Roll S.1
Court records: Curia Regis, Coram Rege, De Banco and Exchequer Rolls to 1290; assize
   rolls and circuit records.
Feudal Documents from the Abbey of Bury (Douglas)

Tudor Town & Country
Wills: Archbishop of Canterbury's court (P.C.C.)—Public Record Office
       Archdeacon of Buckingham's court—Bucks County Record Office
       The Register of Henry Chichele, ed. E. F. Jacob

Civil War
Wills as above
Andrewes letter—Records of Bucks, vii, p.97
Townsmen's claim for damages: Public Record Office SP 28/151
Manorial court records
Waller: Johnson's Lives of the Poets.

Hall Barn
Victoria County History
The History & Antiquities of the County of Buckingham by George Lipscomb, 1847
Records of Buckinghamshire, 1863 to date
Records at Hall Barn and articles and reports by Lady Burnham

Go, Lovely Rose! & Witty and Wise
ed. Thos. W. COPELAND—The Correspondence of Edmund Burke (Nine Volumes) pub.
　　1958-1969. C.U.P. & Chicago.
CHERNAIK—Poetry of Limitation—A study of Edmund Waller. Yale University Press 1968
LLOYD, C.—Waller as a member of the Royal Society. Article in Publications of Mod. Lang.
　　Assn. of America. Vol. XLIII 1928

The Quiet Centuries & From This Day Forth
Primary:　　Muniments Room, Buckinghamshire Archaeological Society
　　　　　　County Record Office
　　　　　　Buckinghamshire County Museum
　　　　　　Buckinghamshire Collection, County Reference Library
　　　　　　Beaconsfield Parish Records
　　　　　　Beaconsfield Congregational Records
　　　　　　Beaconsfield Baptist Records
　　　　　　Beaconsfield Local Board of Health Minutes
　　　　　　Estate Records, Wilton Park, Gregories, Grange
　　　　　　Quit rentals, Manor of Beaconsfield
　　　　　　Bucks CC plans for Beaconsfield District Council offices
　　　　　　Turnpike Acts, 1715, 1719, 1751
　　　　　　Pigot & Co. 1830 Directory
　　　　　　Kelly's Directories for 1865, 1876, 1881, 1887, 1891, 1895, 1899, 1907
　　　　　　Records of Beaconsfield Children's Convalescent Home
　　　　　　Publications of Bekonscot Model Village
　　　　　　County of Buckingham, Calendar to the Sessions Records, 1678-1712.
Secondary:　Records of Buckinghamshire, 1863 to date
　　　　　　Victoria County History
　　　　　　The History & Antiquities of the County of Buckingham
　　　　　　　　by George Lipscomb, 1847
　　　　　　Magna Britannica by Rev. Daniel Lysons, 1806
　　　　　　Stage Coaches and Carriages by L. Sparkes, 1975
　　　　　　Beaconsfield 700th Charter 1269-1969
　　　　　　Beaconsfield UDC Official Guide 1973-4
　　　　　　Beaconsfield District Official Guide 1975

Church of St. Teresa of the Child Jesus & S. Thomas More & John Fisher, Beaconsfield, 1963

A Short History of Beaconsfield & Holtspur United Reformed Church 1704-1974

A History & Guide, Parish Church of St. Mary & All Saints, Beaconsfield

The Site of Burnham Abbey by Sister Jane Mary, S.P.B.

A History of Burnham Abbey, by Sister Jane Mary, S.P.B.

History & Topography of Buckinghamshire by J. J. Sheahan, 1862

Bucks Constabulary Centenary 1857-1957 by Alfred G. Hailstone

The Chiltern Society—The Penn Country Footpath Map 1972

Beaconsfield Old Town Conservation Area Map 1969

Barnett's Street Plan of Beaconsfield and District.

Publications of Beaconsfield & District Historical Society:

Essay on the History of Beaconsfield in "Fair and Festival" Programme   1969

Edith B. Warr—Early Schooldays in Beaconsfield 1854-1914   1968

Kathleen Day—Recollections of Old Beaconsfield   1969

Beaconsfield Parish Registers 1600-1839   1973

Index

147

Subscribers

Presentation copies

1 **Beaconsfield Town Council**
2 **Beaconsfield District Council**
3 **Beaconsfield Library**
4 **Lord Burnham**

5 Gerald Elvey
6 Henry Reed
7 Mrs B. A. Stainton
8 Clive Birch
9 Roy and Susanne Preece
10 The Partners, Gallery 79
11 County Record Office
12 Mrs J. R. Skan
13 Mrs B. A. Stainton
14 E. J. Mosdell
15 A. P. J. Gatward
16 D. Thornton
17 Mrs J. P. Tunnell
18 G. Deakin
19 Mrs Y. Case
20 A. G. Marx
21 W. G. Simpson
22 Hedley J. Meek
23 Mr & Mrs Peter Langley
24 Miss M. Freeston
25 H. B. Naish
26 Mr & Mrs C. M. Wagner
27 Mr & Mrs David Weston Ormond
28 Mr & Mrs Ray Japinga
29 Miss J. H. Chilton
30 Capt & Mrs G. A. Foulds
31 M. R. Boothroyd
32 K. E. Fletcher
33 Miss W. M. Norcross
34 Mrs J. B. Lane
35 P. J. Soutar
36 Mr & Mrs G. S. Planner
37 Miss Patricia Joan Duno
38 Miss Nancy Jean Duno
39 Betty Tucker
40 B. H. Stamp
41 John and Joan Armistead
42 Mr & Mrs J. K. Barker
43 Mr and Mrs R. A. Webber
44 Stephen Calam
45 Mr & Mrs W. D. A. Mills
46 Alfriston School, Knotty Green
47 Simon Barry
48 Robert H. Hatfield
49 Richard E. Portnoy
50 Rosemary A. Ing
51 Bernard C. Frost
52 Mrs M. Finch-Davies
53 Mrs L. E. Kemp
54 D. F. Asher
55 Miss J. Butterman
56 Mr & Mrs P. R. Brierley
57 John Hood
58 Valerie C. Baskwill
59 R. E. S. Bridges
60 W. D. Hoath
61 Mrs A. M. Townsend
62 George W. Gillam
63 P. A. J. Parker
64 T. E. Summers
65 T. E. Oldknow
66 D. G. W. Davis
67 Mrs Geraldine Elson
68 Geoffrey Green
69 Mrs J. Feltham
70 M. W. Puzey
71 A. S. Goldingham
72 David P. Osborn
73 Mr & Mrs R. Long
74 Mrs J. E. Fearol
75 Mrs G. Huggins

76 Mrs J. E. Massey
77 D. E. Collins
78 R. N. J. Barraclough
79 } Dr Nicholas
80 } Temperley
81 Miss E. A. Taylor
82 Mrs R. A. Harden
83 Mrs Wm. C. Chandler
84 Mrs M. L. Lindberg
85 L. A. Lovey
86 R. J. White
87 Mrs C. T. Fossel
88 Mrs H. J. Simmonds
89 R. E. Brown
90 Mrs R. E. Hickox
91 J. E. Francis
92 H. J. Lorton
93 Joyce Griffiths
94 Dr J. W. Pendered
95 Mr & Mrs D. W. Lamb
96 David Routledge
97 Mrs A. E. Pretty
98 D. G. E. Hilton
99 N. H. Tuckley
100 Mr & Mrs A. N. Mills
101 A. I. Suttie
102 B. Hall
103 B. Limbrey
104 V. H. Hughes
105 Mrs B. H. Carr
106 Joanne M. G. Hillestad
107 Mrs Church
108 Robin J. Harper
109 P. J. Howarth
110 Mrs P. K. Heal
111 Mrs A. Sibbald
112 H. C. Bischoff
113 Mr & Mrs J. R. S. Roberts
114 D. G. E. Hilton
115 R. W. Aldeman
116 D. H. Chadwick
117 Donald Spence Furniss
118 W. Haxton
119 Mrs W. H. Hollis
120 A. C. Reeves
121 }
132 } Bucks County Library
133 Colonel L. P. Rose
134 H. J. Rider
135 Yvonne Fitzgerald
136 Mrs H. Manley
137 Roberta Howard
138 Meredith Kurtz
139 Miss P. V. Harford
140 Mrs Barbara V. Martin
141 Mrs J. Pymont
142 Mrs B. Deacon
143 D. T. Wayte
144 Colin le Messurier
145 Mrs S. Appleton
146 Mrs S. Tecke
147 Miss Valerie Pocock
148 Roger C. H. Horne
149 Mrs F. E. White
150 R. Holmes
151 R. L. Bowerman

152 Mrs V. Nash
153 Saint Mary and All Saints Church School
154 Mrs Elizabeth Devereux
155 Alex S. Renton
156 G. V. Hill
157 Mrs C. Gadsdon
158 Miss H. Bishop
159 Paul Honigmann
160 Robert Andrus
161 I. M. Scott
162 G. A. Higham
163 E. N. Kelleher
164 Mrs J. E. Woodcock
165 F. C. Curtis
166 Mrs A. Noyes
167 Mrs S. S. Feasey
168 Miss R. Yates
169 R. F. Smith
170 Beverley Gibson
171 Miss P. J. Paton
172 Mr & Mrs G. Huggins
173 Mrs D. Donnelly
174 Mr & Mrs J. S. Van Zetten
175 Mrs H. A. Orris
176 D. M. Saunders
177 Keith Courtney Marshall
178 Mr & Mrs S. T. Danbury
179 Donald R. Stewart
180 R. A. Raffety
171 Roger N. and Virginia C. Blaker
182 Walter Joseph Craft
183 R. K. Palmer
184 Mr & Mrs E. Smith
185 Mr & Mrs Benyon
186 J. B. Whybrow
187 Miss Ethel Quarman
188 Mr & Mrs Jardine
189 Hylda Edgerley
190 Mrs Ribiki
191 T. Alexander
192 Mrs S. M. Cullinane
193 Mrs S. Modlinger
194 Mrs O. C. McKenzie
195 D. C. Weekes
196 Mrs D. J. Beard
197 Miss Lebon
198 Mrs G. R. Bishop
199 Miss Patricia Macartney
200 Mrs B. J. Rimmer
201 Michael R. Childs
202 K. Favell
203 G. C. Musson
204 Lorna Stoneham
205 E. F. H. Mathison
206 A. J. Frall
207 Mrs M. R. Pelham Burn
208 Mrs M. E. Monro
209 Mrs Nigel Leek
210 M. W. Metcalfe
211 C. H. Woods
212 Dianne Pearson
213 Mrs M. Hearne
214 K. C. Rumens

215 F. Norman J. Reeves
216 Mrs J. M. Wells
217 Mrs J. P. Chase
218 }
219 } Mrs J. Leggett
220 F. D. Leggett
221 Mrs Robert H. Smith
222 Mrs T. S. Johnson
223 Adele Mary Cuthbert
224 Ronald M. Bell QC MP
225 E. J. Winterbotham
226 Ainsley Calderbank
227 Mr & Mrs Vernon Dee Moats
228 Mrs J. E. M. Fogden
229 E. Bruce Ward
230 Rev Nicholas Molony
231 D. J. Woods
232 Marie Williams
233 G. V. P. Vockins
234 J. M. Thomas
235 Mrs D. Arthur
236 J. Oates
237 Mrs J. Randolph
238 D. J. Kean
239 Alan Kitney
240 W. Rademaker
241 A. D. V. Crook
242 Brian F. MacCabe
243 G. L. W. Street
244 Major John M. Macfarlane
245 W. J. Hilliard
246 A. R. Wylie
247 Mrs Patricia Prentice
248 Peter Chard
249 Miss T. E. Vernon
250 } Penn Cottage
252 } Bookshop
253 Mrs J. E. Bryant
254 Carol Sawyer
255 Eric William Baynham
256 C. J. Seabright
257 C. J. Long
258 Mr Powell
259 A. J. Cruickshank
260 Trustee Savings Bank, Beaconsfield
261 L. H. Oates
262 P. C. Colstorm
263 S. C. E. Inchbald FRICS
264 Herbert A. H. Cray
265 C. D. Clarke
266 Joan Wright
267 Gordon Kirby
268 W. A. Matthews
269 Keith R. Drysdale
270 Robert G. Drysdale
271 G. H. Wyatt
272 E. Delplanque
273 E. W. A. Hearne
274 George Bennett Warren
275 D. Spooner
276 J. R. Alcock
277 J. Green
278 Allan P. Simmons
279 Mrs Dorothy E. Parks
280 C. R. Lamb
281 Mr & Mrs E. Morby
282 Mrs B. J. Walker
283 K. G. Walker
284 W. H. Norris
285 Miss E. A. Taylor
286 Stephen and Vicki Wegg-Prosser
287 Raymond W. Birch CBE
288 Malcolm Read
289 David Read
290 F. R. Smith
291 D. Gripper

Remaining names unlisted